CELTIC WARRIORS

CELTIC WARRIORS

The armies of one of the first great peoples in Europe

• DÁITHÍ Ó HÓGÁIN •

THOMAS DUNNE BOOKS

ST. MARTIN'S PRESS ⚏ NEW YORK

A THOMAS DUNNE BOOK
An imprint of St. Martin's Press

Celtic Warriors. Copyright © 1999 by Dáithí ÓhÓgáin.

ISBN 0-312-20509-0

First published in the United Kingdom by Pegasus Publications Ltd.

First US Edition

10-9 8 7 6 5 4 3 2 1

© 1999 Pegasus Publications Ltd
7 St George's Square
London SW1V 2HX
United Kingdom

THE AUTHOR
Dáithí Ó hÓgáin, MA, PhD, is Associate Professor at University College,
Dublin, Ireland, where he lectures on Irish folklore. He is the author of 20 books,
many in Irish, on aspects of folk culture and tradition, and these include six books of
poetry and short stories. He is a well-known conference lecturer, has participated
in the production of documentary films in Europe and the United States, as well as a
frequent radio and TV broadcaster.

Editor: Ray Bonds
Creative Director: John Strange
Designer: Megra Mitchell
Photo research: Tony Moore and Michael Nicholson
Color reproduction: The Emirates Press

PICTURE CREDITS
Front cover: top, Werner Forman Archive; centre, The Bridgeman Art Library; bottom, Werner Forman Archive. Back cover: top, British Museum; Page 1:Via Michael Nicholson 3: AKG Photo London/Erich Lessing.5: British Museum. 8 and 9: AKG Photo London/Erich Lessing. 10: top and bottom, AKG Photo London/Erich Lessing. 12: R Sheridan/Ancient Art & Architecture Collection. 13: via Michael Nicholson. 14: via Cork University Press/Routledge. 15: Mitteregger Photographenteam. 16: R Sheridan/Ancient Art & Architecture Collection. 19: R Sheridan/Ancient Art & Architecture Collection. 20: R Sheridan/Ancient Art & Architecture Collection. 21: top, AKG Photo London/Erich Lessing; bottom, R Sheridan/Ancient Art & Architecture Collection. 22: AKG Photo London/Erich Lessing. 23: via Michael Nicholson. 25: AKG Photo London/Erich Lessing. 28: AKG Photo London. 29: Peter Newark's Military Pictures. 30: AKG Photo London. 31: R Sheridan/Ancient Art & Architecture Collection. 32: R Sheridan/Ancient Art & Architecure Collection. 33: AKG Photo London. 34. AKG Photo London/Erich Lessing. 35: e.t. archive. 37: AKG Photo London/Erich Lessing. 39: F H C Birch/Sonia Halliday Photographs. 41: top and bottom, AKG Photo London/Erich Lessing. 42: Michael Nicholson. 45. Michael Nicholson. 46-47: AKG Photo London/Erich Lessing. 49: from Museo Nazionale Romano.. 50: R Sheridan/Ancient Art & Architecture Collection. 51: AKG Photo London/Erich Lessing. 53: AKG Photo London. 55: top and bottom, via Michael Nicholson. 56: AKG Photo London/Erich Lessing. 57: National Museum of Ireland. 58: AKG Photo London/Erich Lessing. 59: via Michael Nicholson. 60: AKG Photo London. 63: via Michael Nicholson. 65: : via Michael Nicholson. 66-67 and 68: R Sheridan/Ancient Art & Architecture Collection. 70-71: AKG Photo London/Erich Lessing. 72: British Museum. 73: R Sheridan/Ancient Art & Architecture. 74: top, Gabinetto Fotografico/Soprintendenza Archeologica per la Toscana, Firenze. 78-79: AKG Photo London/Erich Lessing. 80: Werner Forman Archive. 81: Trip/Ask Images. 82: Michael Nicholson. 84-85: British Museum. 86: Michael Nicholson. 89: Hampshire County Museum Service. 90: via Michael Nicholson. 91: Michael Nicholson. 93: Society of Antiquaries of London. 94: British Museum. 95: top, Bibliotheque Nationale de France; bottom, R Sheridan/Ancient Art & Architecture Collection. 97-100: British Museum. 101: J Beecham/Ancient Art & Architecture Collection. 102: via Michael Nicholson. 103: Michael Nicholson. 106: British Museum. 107: Collections/Fay Godwin. 108-109: Hampshire County Museum Service. 110: British Museum. 111: Michael Nicholson. 112: top, Michael Nicholson. 114: Aerofilms. 115: Collections/Michael St Maur Sheil.

Please note that the publishers have made every effort to trace the copyright owners of all images reproduced in this book, and apologise to any of those they may have been unable to trace and ask that they make contact with them at the address shown.

CONTENTS

PREFACE

The Celts were one of the most important population groups in ancient Europe. The power of the Celtic peoples expanded greatly for some centuries, and then contracted to an even greater degree, so that their civilisation almost disappeared. Only in the west did their culture survive, and Celtic languages are still spoken in Ireland, Scotland, Wales and Brittany. Manx and Cornish are two other recently spoken Celtic languages, and attempts are being made at the revival of these.

The book does not treat of the period of written Celtic sources, native literature having begun in Ireland in the 6th Century AD and in Wales soon afterwards. For the early history of the Celts we are therefore dependent on Greek and Latin literature, supplemented by information gleaned from archaeological studies. Since the Greeks and Romans were in conflict with the Celts, the accounts which have come down to us are almost all of a hostile character, and this should be borne in mind. If we had accounts from the Celts themselves of their early history, these would surely alter the historical data to no small extent.

As it is, our only approach can be to present the available information in systematic form, and to attempt to analyse this so as to get a picture of what the general situation was. The picture which emerges is in many ways a sad and tragic one, but it is an essential component of the history of Europe, and it provides a vista on an aspect of European heritage which is not widely known.

The description is as specific as circumstances allow, with an attempt to follow a chronological pattern. Names of Celtic personages are generally given in the forms attested by the Greek and Latin writers, which do not always accord exactly with the actual pronunciation used by the Celts themselves. The symbol * indicates forms of words which are not directly attested, but which have been reconstructed from comparative linguistics. A detailed list of Celtic groups in antiquity, with explanations of their names and references to their locations (where known), can be found in the Appendix and the end of the book.

Dáithí Ó hÓgáin,
um Earrach na bliana 1999
(in the Spring of 1999)

And the tall men
and the swordsmen
and the horsemen,
where are they?

W B Yeats

Chapter I

WHO WERE THE CELTS?

rchaeological remains provide our only clues to the peoples who inhabited the Europe of several thousands of years ago, and to the kinds of lives which they led. As the Stone Age drew to a conclusion at the beginning of the 2nd Millennium BC, a variety of population groups inhabited that large area, with no doubt a range of different languages and cultures. The spread and contraction of these populations was influenced not least by new influxes of peoples from the east, and the most notable of these must have been the speakers of dialects which scholars term 'Indo-European' - that is, dialects of a language which at some stage in the ancient world originated somewhere on the southern border of Europe and Asia and was spreading eastwards and south-eastwards into Asia and westwards into Europe.

ABOVE: Dagger and sheath
from the 6th Century BC. The
handle of the dagger and the
sheath are gold-coated. Found
at Hallstatt; now in the
Naturhistorisches Museum,
Vienna.

These peoples were the first users of bronze in Europe, and their most developed groups were the Hittite empire in Asia Minor, and the Minoan-Mycenaean civilisation of the Aegean. From them the use of bronze spread gradually into all areas of Europe and, as the power of these two peoples declined towards the end of the 2nd Millennium, the archaeological record shows the growth in wealth and prestige of other groups in the centre of the Continent. One of these groups were the 'Tumulus People', so called from the impressive barrows which they built over their dead leaders, and who were domiciled in the area immediately north of the Alps. In a broad area to the north of these again were the 'Urnfield People', who cremated their dead and placed the bones in urns. Around the year 1,000 BC the cultures of these two peoples joined in the Danube Basin, and from there spread into the whole area from the Carpathian Mountains in the east to the Atlantic in the west. The Urnfield People would appear to have been the dominant element in this amalgam, and it is therefore likely that their dialect was also the more influential. This new amalgam, at any rate, must represent the origin of the people whom we know as Celts, for the early Greek writers used the designation *Keltoi* for the population of that general area.

That these were a war-like people is evidenced by the number of weapons, particularly swords, which they buried with their dead; and this probably accounts for their name also. In common with the other ascendant groups in Europe at the time, they were speakers of an Indo-European dialect, and comparative linguistics indicate that the designation *Keltoi* comes from an Indo-European root **kel-* (meaning 'to strike'). Thus, the word **keld-* would have meant 'fighter', giving the cognates *hilta* ('combat') in Germanic and *clades* ('destroyer') in Latin. The original meaning of the term Celts would therefore appear to have been 'warriors', and would have been used by themselves as a laudatory term reflecting their success in overcoming other peoples and spreading their power. Their military concerns are also reflected by the large amount of hill-forts constructed and maintained by them. These fortifications must have been intended more for maintaining power over local subjects than for security against attack by marauding strangers.

The perspectives of these early Celts are also evident from their burials. Combinations of bronze cremation urns with bronze swords represent the burials of chieftains, while the remains of four-wheeled wagons and fine pottery would indicate a belief in a journey to be undertaken to the afterlife. This complex is most clearly represented in a grave-chamber at Hart an-der-Alz in Upper Bavaria, dating from the 10th Century BC. Burials within large tumuli soon came to the fore as a special distinction for very powerful lords, and by the 8th Century BC weapons of iron began to appear. The most celebrated burials of this kind were discovered at Hallstatt, by a lakeside in the mountains of Upper Austria, but there are many other examples — dating to the 7th and 6th Centuries BC — from Bohemia, southern Germany, Switzerland, and the south-east of France. In these, the body is not burnt, but lies on a wagon—often within a specially constructed wooden chamber. The dead leader is furnished with iron swords and spears, as well as pottery, cups, knives, and joints of beef and pork. The latter items show that it was believed that he would continue to feast in the afterlife.

LEFT: Bronze face-mask with
punctuate decoration (width
9.06in/23cm) and two bronze-
foil hands (length 6.10in/
15.5cm and 5.51in/15cm)
from the Hallstatt period, 7th
Century BC. Found
respectively at Kleinklein,
Styria, and Kroell
Schmidkogel; now in
Landesmuseum Johanneum,
Steiermark, Austria.

The increasing centralisation of power within strong kindred groups is indicated by multiple burials in tumuli at this time. These had elaborate grave-goods, including women's ornaments. One particularly notable burial was that of a woman of about thirty-five years of age, apparently a princess, at Châtillon-sur-Seine in central eastern France. Within a large tumulus, her body was laid out on a wagon, with a golden diadem on her head, and the grave included also a finely engraved bronze vessel of Greek origin, as well as bracelets and brooches.

By the 6th Century BC, the long swords had become less common in burials, and in their place we find spears and daggers with richly worked hilts. These large tumuli were often situated at some distance from groups of smaller tumuli, and nearer to hillforts, from which we can deduce that the chieftains were developing a cult which linked the current power structures with inherited prestige.

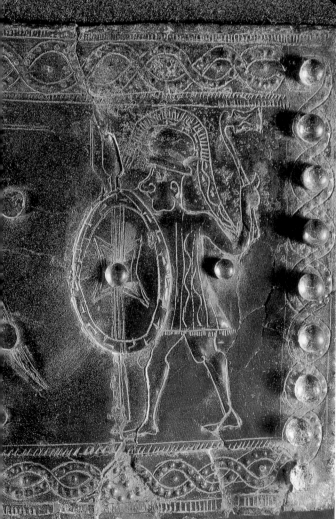

There is evidence, also, of an increase in the importation of prestige goods from the Mediterranean cultures. Bronze weapons, as well as helmets and leg-armour from Greece were in high demand among the Celts. These were mostly imported through the Greek colony, which had been established at Massilia (Marseilles) since the 7th Century BC, before the arrival of the Celts in that area. Elaborate pottery was also acquired from that source, as well as beaked flagons of high quality and other bronze utensils got from the Etruscans to the south. Along with such ware, the most significant import was wine, which would have been used for aristocratic feasts. The upper classes of the Celts soon developed a fine taste for wine, as is clear from Classical sources. Commerce over the Alpine passes flourished in the 5th Century BC, and for their part the Celts traded cattle, slaves, and apparently also gold—which was readily available to the most powerful families from alluvial deposits on the banks of the Rhine, the Danube and the Otava.

Iron had been available since the 8th Century BC, and its use for weapons gradually increased. Iron gave a distinct advantage to its possessors, and it is thought indeed that the Germanic peoples borrowed their word for iron from the Celtic *isarnon (meaning 'hard metal'). There was an increase also in the use of gold and silver for artistic decoration. By the 5th Century BC a whole range of new designs, both aesthetic and functional, were developing as the Celts learned from other peoples and developed their own master-smiths and workshops. This is known as the La Tène era, from the discovery of a large collection of such products at a village of that name in western Switzerland.

These cultural advances had their own importance, not only in terms of prestige, but also in terms of power-politics. For instance, whereas ordinary four-wheeled wagons had been in general use for a long time, an increased use of bronze and iron parts, added to rich decorations, now adorned special wagons for ceremonial use. To render travel and transport more convenient, iron tyres were now being affixed to the wheels of wagons, and eventually the fast two-wheeled chariots for use in fighting were developed. Large iron-working centres were established, and these produced - in addition to weapons—a wide variety of tools which greatly increased the technical capacity of the Celtic peoples. Increasing power, wealth, and efficiency were thus the hallmarks of the Celts in their native central European area.

The homeland of the Celts in the 6th Century BC covered a huge area including eastern France, all of Switzerland, most of Austria, southern Germany, Bohemia, and adjacent areas. The balance of power between their ancient kings and chieftains must have fluctuated somewhat, but by the 5th Century BC the three strongest centres were the Marne region in the north-west, the Moselle region to the east of that, and Bohemia furthest east. From later sources, we can identify the leading tribes who inhabited these and other regions. The Aedui were in Marne, with the Aulerci to the west of them and the Senones, Bituriges, Carnutes and Arverni to the south; the Belgae, Mediomatrici and Treveri were in the Moselle region; and the Volcae in Bohemia, with the largest section of the Boii on the borders of Celtdom in the extreme east.

ABOVE LEFT: Warriors with large rounded shields probably of the Veneti people, whose territory lay directly south of the Alpine Celts. Detail from bronze situla, zone-height (2.17in / 5.5cm). Found at Este, Villa Benvenuti, Venice – tomb number 126 (formerly 73).

BELOW LEFT: Warrior, probably a Celt, with lance and large rounded shield, from the Hallstatt period (5th Century BC). Detail from a rectangular belt fragment of bronze, found at Vace in Slovenia. Now at Naturhistorisches Museum, Vienna.

RIGHT: The extent of Celtic power in Europe at the beginning of the 5th Century BC.

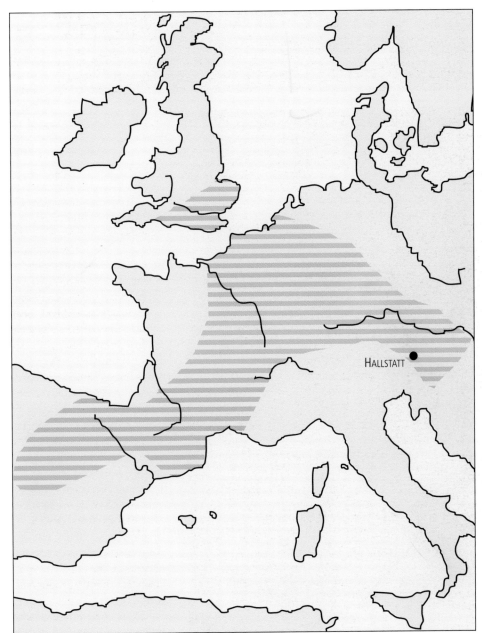

HALLSTATT

Bronze helmet found at Blainville, near Nantes in the west of France. It may have belonged to a warrior of one of the Bronze Age peoples who were displaced by the expanding Celts.

To the south of all these, and verging on the Alps, were tribes such as the Lingones, Sequani and Helvetii. Due to the general Celtic tendency towards movement, sections of several tribes would have been found in different areas—for instance, the Volcae had sections in both the south of France and Bohemia. Smaller groups had also developed, such as the Menapii and Morini on the north-eastern coast of France, the Armorici and the Osissmii in the direction of Brittany, and the Cadurci, Gabali, and Vellavi in the south of France. Finally, there were tribes in the south-east towards Marseilles who appear to have been a mixed population of Celts and Ligurians, tribes such as the Saluvii and the Turoni.

The first written references to the Celts come from an account in Greek of a voyage by Himilco, who sailed around part of the Atlantic coast, shortly before the year 530 BC. He was a Carthaginian, who had been commissioned by the recently established Greek colony at Marseilles to explore the sea-routes for them as far as the city of Tartessos (in the vicinity of the Gulf of Cadiz). There his crew had been told that the Tartessians had actually travelled north along the Atlantic coast, and one of the crew left an account of this. The account survives in fragmentary form in the text of a Latin poem written many centuries later, but there are several additions in this, which we can take to be from a rewriting of the Greek text in the 4th Century BC. The surviving account, then, can properly be related only to the situation at that later time, but even in this form it gives a few—albeit obscure—insights into the prehistory of western Europe.

The view of western Europe given in it is much condensed. It is clear that France is taken to be much shorter from south to north than it really is, and accordingly the English Channel is taken to be a virtual continuation of the Bay of Biscay, which in turn is almost synonymous with the Atlantic coast of Spain. Various peoples are mentioned as inhabiting this greatly convoluted region, such as the 'Cynetes', the 'Saefi', the 'Cempses', and the 'Ligures'. The islands beyond (including Britain, whose product of tin is mentioned) are referred to as the 'Oestrymnides', and the area of Brittany and western France in general is called 'Oestrymnis'. It would appear that all these references are to indigenous Bronze Age populations who were feeling, or beginning to feel, the pressure of the expanding Celts.

A hint at ongoing conquest and displacement of peoples may be given by the reference to how the Oestrymnii tilled the soil of their country, but 'after many years a serpent made the cultivators flee'. This may be a play on an old Celtic tribe or group, 'Saefes', which would call to mind the Greek word 'sepes' (meaning 'snakes'). A definite reference to such displacement occurs in a passage on the Ligures, whose land is said to be 'tenantless now, and wasted long by bands of Celts and by many a bloody foray'. These Ligures, it is claimed, had been put to flight by such raids and had retreated as far as the North Sea! This could be a confused memory of how the Celts, in their expansion, had pushed the Ligurians from some territory inhabited by them in central France. The Ligurians did actually survive, not only in north-west Italy, but also in the south-east of France.

The position vis-à-vis Britain and Ireland at the time is more difficult to decipher from the text. Regarding Britain, the following reference is strikingly accurate:

> *Other coasts some distance off, braving the north wind's frosty blast, tower over the waters with their mighty cliffs—twin cliffs they are, with their rich soil clothed in spreading sward, stretching to where in the turbid western sea the Rhine is hidden...*

The reference is obviously to the Cliffs of Dover. It was these white cliffs which gave its ancient name to the island, and that name is indeed cited in the Latin text, viz. 'the broad isle of the Albiones'. Ireland is referred to as being 'peopled thickly by the Hierni'. These two population names are easily recognisable from early Irish literature, from the toponyms 'Ériu' (from Celtic *Everiu) for Ireland and 'Albu' (from Celtic *Albiu) for Britain. But there are some difficulties. Firstly, it is not altogether certain that the names were Celtic in origin and, even if they were, from the reference to them it would appear that the information came from Celts on the European mainland. This cannot therefore be taken to indicate that the two islands themselves were inhabited by Celts before the 4th Century BC.

We can, however, be sure, that the names Ierne and Albion soon became current in Greek for the two islands, for they were thus referred to a century later by Eratosthenes. Pytheas of Marseilles, who visited Britain about 325 BC, may also have been acquainted with the same toponymics, but he collectively called the countries the 'Prettanik' islands. This was derived from the population name *Pritani*, which gave rise to the Latin *Britannia* and the Welsh *Prydein*. The new name indicates that a significant part of Britain was at that time under the control of the people who bore it, and there can hardly be any doubt but that these Pritani were Celts. They had probably begun to arrive in Britain from the European Continent as early as the 5th Century BC, carrying with them some iron weapons and tools. The designation Pritani itself - like Albion - would appear to have been first applied to the inhabitants of the island by Continental Celts. In referring to the Cliffs of Dover, the surviving Latin version of the 'Himilco' text states that 'upon their bosoms dread bands of *Britanni* live'. There may indeed have been bands of Pritani already settled in the south-east of the island at the time, but this is the Latin variant of their name and must be considered a late interpolation.

It is logical to suggest, then, that in the 5th Century BC the habitat of the Celts was expanding rapidly, from a broad sward of central Europe as far as the Atlantic in the west and touching on the English Channel in the north. They had become strongly entrenched in the south-west as far as the Pyrenees but had as yet not occupied land south and immediately west of the Alps. The further their power stretched, the looser the connections would

Modern illustration of a hunter-warrior on horseback, with helmet and long spear and accompanied by dog, intended to depict life in the period when the Celts were beginning to expand their power. (Painting by F Corman.)

Outdoor cooking-pit from ancient Ireland. Stones were heated in the fire and then dropped into the water-trough, which was brought to the boil in this way. Reproduced from Seán P Ó Riordáin, Antiquities of the Irish Countryside *(Cork University Press, Routledge, 1942).*

have become between their various groups, but the vanguard of their development was shifting from the area of Bohemia and Austria to that of south-western Germany and southern France. This situation is reflected by the Greek writer Hecataeus, around the year 500 BC, who referred to *Narbon* (Narbonne) as *empórion kai pólis Keltiké* ('a market and city of the Celts'). Over a hundred years later Herodotus declared that the river Danube rises in the country of the *Keltoi* in the west.

It is obvious however that, to these early writers, the Celts were little more than a fascinating race, concerning whom garbled and sensationalised accounts could be gained from traders and mariners. Thus, the great dramatist Aeschylus used the somewhat fantastic name Hyperboreans (*Uperboreoi*, 'far-northerners') for them, and his contemporary Hellanicus claimed that they were a very just people who ate acorns and other fruit rather than meat. As late as the 4th Century BC, Ephorus could claim that the Celts were 'very careful to avoid growing fat or big-bellied' and that 'if any young man exceeds the measure of a certain girdle he is fined'.

Tall-tales circulating among the Greeks were not all so complimentary to the Celts. References made to them by Aristotle are somewhat ambiguous, as when he praises them for their courage, but expresses the opinion that in this they were rash to the point of madness. He further claimed that they plunged their new-born children into a cold stream, clothed only in a light wrapper, in order to make them healthy.

Their sexual mores, too, he considered dubious, saying that they 'openly approve of connexion with the male'. This charge, though hardly sustainable, was repeated in dramatic terms several centuries later by Posidonius: 'Although their wives are beautiful, they pay very little attention to them, but rather have a strange passion for the embraces of males. Their custom is to sleep on the ground upon the skins of wild animals and to wallow among bedfellows on each side. The strangest thing of all is that, without a thought of keeping up proper appearances, they carelessly yield their virginity to others; and this they regard not as a disgrace, but rather think themselves slighted when someone refuses to accept their freely offered favours.'

To such writers, the Celts could be portrayed as the opposite of the civilised Greeks in whatever way was opportune to mention. In this vein, Aristotle's teacher Plato wrote of the Celts as one of those war-like peoples who contrasted with the abstemious Greeks in drinking wine to the point of 'downright drunkenness'. There may of course be some truth behind this, as there definitely seems to be behind Aristotle's own statement that the Celts were perturbed by 'neither earthquakes nor waves'. This was apparently a proverbial expression used by the Celts themselves in boasting of their courage.

A generation or two later, Ptolemy, son of Lagus, who was a lieutenant of Alexander the Great, gave an anecdote concerning the Celts who dwelt on the Adriatic. Their ambassadors came to Alexander in order to secure a treaty of goodwill and friendship. They were cordially received and, while drinking, were asked by Alexander what they feared most of all - expecting, of course, that they would diplomatically say that they feared him. But they replied that they feared no man, but that they were worried lest the sky might perhaps fall on top of them.

One version of this anecdote has the Celtic envoys adding a diplomatic note to their bravado, by having them say that 'they valued above everything the friendship of so great a man as he'. Another version may be more illustrative of their real mentality, however, when it states that they made the unexpected reply in full awareness that they 'lived far away in lands difficult of access, and had perceived that Alexander's expedition at that time was destined for other parts'. Their attitude left a wry taste in the mouth of the great conqueror, for 'having addressed them as friends and made them allies he dismissed them, and afterwards expressed his opinion that the Celts were braggarts'.

This martial proverb gave rise to other traditions about the Celts. Ephorus, for instance, claimed that the Celts, as an exercise of their intrepidity, allowed their houses to be washed away by flood-tides and were satisfied to rebuild later, and that 'a greater number of them perish by water than by war'. Later texts refer to 'the Celts, who take up arms against the waves of the sea' and to how they resist the tides with their swords in their hands, till they perish in the waters, 'in order that they may not seem to fear death by taking the precaution to flee'. Such a portrayal, though inaccurate, may have derived from some real occurrence, such as a report of an inundation of land held by the Celts, possibly in the Netherlands.

Rumours aside, the courage and ferocity of the Celts in battle can hardly be doubted and - as we shall see in later chapters—this led to great demand for their warriors as mercenaries in the armies of other nationalities. The Classical writers are copious on the topic, and Posidonius

A decorated bowl, mounted on a cart, and with several figures – all in bronze – found near a cremation urn at Strettweg, in Styria, Austria. It dates to the 7th Century BC, and the cart is 13.78in (35cm) long. The figures on the cart represent a goddess, surrounded by horsemen and footsoldiers. The scene seems to depict the sacrifice of a stag, and the bowl may have been used to collect such sacrificial blood. Now at Landesmuseum Joanneum, Gratz, Austria.

could declare that the whole Celtic race was 'madly fond of war, high-spirited and quick to battle'. He went on:

> When they are stirred up they assemble in their bands for battle, quite openly and without forethought, so that they are easily handled by those who desire to outwit them; for at any time or place on whatever pretext you stir them up, you will have them ready to face danger, even if they have nothing on their side but their own strength and courage... Their strength depends on their mighty bodies, and on their numbers.

This Posidonius was writing in the beginning of the 1st Century BC, and his work survives only in fragments cited by later writers. He undoubtedly had a good knowledge of the Celts of his own time, and there are indications that several of his comments are based on views which had long been held by the Greeks concerning these people. He has this to say of their armoury and weaponry:

> Their armour includes man-sized shields, decorated in individual fashion. Some of these have projecting bronze animals of fine workmanship which serve for defence as well as decoration. On their heads they wear bronze helmets which have large projecting figures, giving the appearance of enormous stature to the wearer. In some cases horns form one piece with the helmet, while in other cases it is relief figures of the fore-parts of birds or quadrupeds. Their trumpets also are of a peculiar barbaric kind—when they blow into them they produce a harsh sound which suits the tumult of war. Some have iron breastplates of chain-mail, while others fight naked, and for them the breastplate provided by nature suffices. Instead of the short sword they carry long swords held by iron or bronze chains and hanging along their right flank. Some wear gold-plaited or silver-plaited belts around their tunics. The spears which they brandish in battle, and which they call lanciae, have iron heads a cubit or more in length and a little less than two palms in breadth. Their swords are as long as the javelins of other peoples, and their javelins have points longer than swords. Some of their javelins are forged with a straight head, while some are spiral with breaks throughout their entire length, so that the blow not only cuts but also tears the flesh, and the recovery of the spear tears open the wound.

Concerning the physical appearance of the Celts, they were 'tall in stature' and their skin was 'very moist and white'. Their hair was generally blonde, but they also used artificial means to attain this colour. 'They continually wash their hair with lime and draw it back from the forehead to the crown and to the nape of the neck'. Some shaved their beards, while others cultivated a short beard. The nobles shaved the cheeks but let a moustache grow freely so that it covered the mouth, 'and so when they are eating, the moustache becomes entangled in the food, and when they are drinking the liquid passes, as it were, through a sort of strainer'. Regarding their clothing, he has this to say:

> They accumulate large quantities of gold and make use of it for personal ornament, not only the women but also the men. For they wear bracelets on wrists and arms, and around their necks thick rings of solid gold, and they wear also fine finger-rings and even golden tunics... They wear a striking kind of clothing—tunics dyed in various colours, and trousers which they call by the name of bracae, and they wear striped cloaks, fastened with buckles, thick in winter and light in summer, picked out with a variegated small check pattern.

Posidonius was fascinated by the eating habits of the Celts. He claims that they strewed the ground with the skins of wolves or dogs, and sat on these—without any chairs—when dining. The food was served on low wooden tables, and consisted of some loaves and boiled or roasted meat. 'They partake of this in a clean but leonine fashion, raising up whole limbs in both hands and biting off the meat, while any part which is hard to tear off they cut with a small dagger which hangs attached to their sword-sheath in its own scabbard.' Their youngest grown-up children, both boys and girls, tended to them at table. Beside them were blazing charcoal hearths, with cauldrons and spits containing large joints of meat. Those who lived beside a river or sea ate baked fish, with salt, vinegar and cumin. They concocted drinks out of barley and honey and cumin, and when they became drunk they fell into 'a stupor or a maniacal state'.

Then Posidonius mentions a striking feature of their culture, the heroic feast presided over by a king or chieftain. We have seen how this royal feasting was reflected in their ancient burials, and here we have a description of the ceremonial in real life:

> *When a large number dine together they sit around in a circle with the most influential man in the centre, like the leader of a chorus—whether he surpasses the others in skill at war, or in nobility of family, or in wealth. Beside him sits the host, and next on either side the others in order of distinction. Their shieldmen stand behind them, while their spearmen are situated in a circle on the opposite side and feast in common with their leaders. The servers bear around the drink in terracotta or silver jars like spouted cups. The trenchers on which they serve the food are also of these materials, while with others they are made of bronze or are woven or wooden baskets.*

More dramatic scenes of action sometimes followed, if Posidonius is to be credited, for when feasting these Celtic warriors were wont to be moved by chance remarks to wordy disputes, and the irritations could increase to the point of fighting. This was regarded as the result of an ancient ritual concerning precedence:

> *In former times, when the hindquarters were served up, the bravest hero took the thigh piece, and if another man claimed it they stood up and fought in single combat to the death.*

As a form of military drill, the Celts also had the custom of engaging in mock-battles. Posidonius describes this as 'mutual thrust and parry', but states that wounds were sometimes inflicted 'and the irritation caused by this may lead even to the slaying of the opponent unless the bystanders hold them back'. Several reports represent the Celts as engaging in duels, and their fighting ideals were expressed in the most committed form in actual war, in which they considered it a glory to die and a disgrace to survive without victory. They regarded it as the utmost disgrace to desert their leader, and after the fall of a leader they were wont to retire from a battle. The bodies of those slain in battle were often left to the carrion-crows to devour, in the belief that in this way they were taken by the deities, and the war-goddess was believed by them to appear in the form of such a bird.

The Generous Disposition of the Celts

The Classical writers stress that the Celts were generous by disposition, and were wont to invite strangers to their feasts, and only after the meal did they enquire after their identity or business. Julius Caesar, apparently quoting Posidonius, states that 'violation of guest-friendship they regard as impious - strangers who have visited them for whatever reason they protect from injury and hold sacred, and every man's house lies open and his food is shared with them'. Caesar also would have us believe that factionalism was general among the Celts, and that leaders of such factions had the right of final decision in all matters concerning their followers. The faction-leaders would not tolerate their clients being oppressed or defrauded for, if they did, they would lose their own influence and position. The reason why, Caesar says, 'this institution was established of old' was to ensure that 'no common man should lack aid against one more powerful'.

A stress is also put on co-operation among the Celts in the account given by another writer, Strabo, in his discussion of the attitude to war among them. He attributes a straightforward and slightly naive character to them, and claims that 'they assemble in large numbers on slight provocation, being ever ready to sympathise with the anger of a neighbour who thinks he has been wronged'. This surely was a misunderstanding by Strabo of traditions binding tribes and

Life-size sandstone figure which originally stood on a burial mound at Hirschlanden, near Stuttgart. It dates from the 5th Century BC, and the headwear, collar, and belt indicate that the figure was modelled on a Celtic noble of the Hallstatt culture. Now at Römisch-Germanisches Zentral-museum, Mainz, Germany.

families together. Another comment of his makes it clear, however, that social authority could be rather fluid in such situations: 'Most of their governments used to be aristocratic, and in ancient times they used to elect one leader annually, and in the same way one man was declared general by the people to lead in war.'

Another ancient practice of the Celts is referred to by Julius Caesar, who seems here again to have been quoting Posidonius:

> In peace-time they have no public magistrate, but the regional and village chieftains give legal judgements to their people and seek solutions to their disputes. Brigandage outside the state territory brings no disgrace, and they assert that it is pursued in order to exercise their young men and save them from idleness. When a chieftain in council says that he will lead a foray and asks for followers, those who approve of the man and his project rise to support him and promise their help, and are applauded by the assembly. Those who fail to keep their promise are looked on as deserters and traitors, and they are henceforth trusted in nothing.

This passage refers to the custom known in Ireland as fianas, according to which young men learned the trade of a warrior by living outside of normal social rules and surviving on their skill and strength in raiding other groups. It is attested as a custom among many ancient peoples, including the early Greeks and Germans, and it is clear from this passage that it was a recognised aspect of early Celtic society also.

Not all the accounts given by the Classical authors are so credible, however. Pytheas was an accomplished mariner and explorer, who in the 4th Century BC sailed from Marseilles around the Spanish coast, and then northwards by France to Britain, and perhaps even further. Notwithstanding this, he felt it safe to portray the Celts as an exotic people of the imagination like the Hyperboreans. Though his comments on these strange denizens of the north-west cannot be trusted, Pytheas may nevertheless at times have been echoing truths, as when he declares that they used to point out to him where the sun sleeps.

Celtic Belief in 'Otherwold' Island

The ancient Greeks, from Homer onwards, spoke of an otherworld island in the west, situated where the sun goes down. They knew it as Elysion or Erytheia, and it was thought to exist somewhere west of the Gates of Gibraltar. It was thought of, among other things, as a sepulchral island on which stood the pillars of Hercules or the pillars of Cronus. It could be somewhere near Cadiz, a region rich in megalithic tombs, or off the western coast of France. There is evidence that the Celts had the same notion, and that they believed that that island was the abode of the dead. Plutarch, in the 1st century AD, using information which he had from a traveller, describes how the Britons believed that an otherworld lord reigns in slumber over an island off the coast. Boatmen were awakened at night by a knock on their door, and were required to row the spirits of the dead there. It may well be, then, that Pytheas had heard from the Celts that the otherworld lies on a sunlit island in the western sea.

Reports of this kind concerning the religious beliefs of the Celts led the imaginations of Classical writers to run riot concerning strange islands inhabited by even stranger people in the Celtic mist. Posidonius, for instance, wrote that there was a small island at the mouth of the Loire, which was inhabited by women who performed Bacchic rites and made ritual sacrifices to the gods:

> No man is permitted to land on the island; and when the women desire to have intercourse with the other sex, they cross the sea, and afterwards return again. They have a custom of once a year unroofing the whole of the temple, and roofing it again the same day before sunset, each one bringing some of the materials. If any one lets her burden fall, she is torn to pieces by the others, and her limbs carried around the temple with wild shouts, which they never cease until their rage is exhausted. It always happens that some one drops her burden, and is thus sacrificed.

It may be that Posidonius—or his source—had heard something concerning worship of deities by women in the north-western Celtic area, but the portrayal of the raging women with psychotic behaviour is typical of images of 'savages' as seen through 'civilised' eyes.

Stone heads from a Celto-Ligurian shrine dating from the 3rd Century BC at Entremont, Bouche-du-Rhone, in the south of France. The expressions are so striking and individualistic that it is easy to believe that they were modelled on real people in that area. Now in Musée Granet, Aix-en-Provence.

Later still, Pomponius Mela refers to a tradition of another island, called Sena, 'opposite to the shores of the Osissmii' (i.e. between Britain and north-west France). This, he says, was famed for its oracle of a Celtic god, to whose cult nine maiden-priestesses were devoted. These priestesses were known as Senae, and were said to be 'gifted with remarkable intelligence'. It was believed that 'they can raise up the waves of the sea and the winds with their songs, that they can assume the shape of any animal they choose, that they can cure complaints that to others are incurable, and that they know and predict the future'.

This reads curiously parallel to the later accounts of Celtic druids, who were reputed to chant magical poems which controlled the waters, to go abroad in the form of different animals, to cure ailments, and to prophesy. It is apparent that Pytheas had heard something of such wise men of the Celts, and also accounts of women with similar functions, and that he confused these with the Greek legend of Circe, who lived with her nymphs on the island of Ea and could command the winds, change men into the shape of beasts, and foretell the future.

The identity of the island is doubtful. Its name Sena would have meant in Celtic 'the ancient [goddess]'. It may well be that the ultimate source of Pomponius's strange island was the prehistoric cult of a water-goddess. There is plenty of evidence for such river-goddesses

Gilded bronze helmet of the 4th Century BC from Amfreville, near Eure in Normandy. The bronze is overlaid with iron and with decorated gold sheet, and the lower section is inlaid with red enamel. Now in Musée des Antiquités Nationales, Saint-Germain-en-Laye, France.

among the Celts, who tended to give female names to their rivers. For instance, the Danube appears to be synonymous with an ancient goddess Danu (literally 'she of the water'), and the name of the river Marne comes from a Celtic *Matrona* (literally 'divine mother'); while various rivers in the Celtic world bore the name *Deva* ('goddess'). That such cults existed among the Celts is further suggested by a report of Artemidorus in the 2nd Century BC of 'an island near Britain' where sacrifices were offered to goddesses.

Among the Celts, rivers were thought of as being a principal fertilising aspect of the land-goddess, on whom they depended for food and sustenance and to whom various designations were given. These designations appear to have varied from group to group and from locality to locality, but included such as Brigenti ('the highest one'), Damona ('the divine cow'), Epona

ABOVE: The celebrated cauldron found in a bog at Gundestrup in Jutland, Denmark. It is 27.56in (70cm) in diameter, and is believed to have come from a Celtic workshop in eastern Europe early in the 1st Century BC. Made of chased silver plates, its elaborate range of figures seems to represent a fusion of mythology and ritual. Now in the Nationalmuseet, Copenhagen.

RIGHT: Iron sword with bronze hilt from the 3rd Century BC, France. Its design combines utility and decoration.

('the divine mare'), Nantosuelta ('the flowing stream'). Often she was paired with a male deity, and the origin of this would appear to be the coupling of the male sky with the female earth so as to ensure fruitfulness. The basic name for the male sun-deity among the Celts must have been *dago-Devos ('the good god'), the second part of whose name is the Celtic version of the general Indo-European sky-god *Deiwos. Among other male-deities, who apparently were derivations of this same being, were Taranis ('the thunderer'), Sucellus ('the striker'), Ekwomaros or Epomaros ('the great stallion'), Esus ('the good lord'), and Cernunnos ('the horned one').

That the sun was the ultimate father and the earth the ultimate mother of the people was a

doctrine of the wise men of the Celts. It is clear from the Classical writers that they divided these learned men of theirs into three grades, a member of each grade being known respectively as *bardos, vátis,* and *druis.* The *bardi* were 'singers and poets', the *vátes* were 'interpreters of sacrifice', and the *druides* were experts in 'the science of nature'. We may assume, however, that this was a somewhat pedagogic division, and that in practice the functions were often combined in one individual practitioner. There is evidence, in fact, that another term was also in use for such a wise man or religious leader, namely *velitos, meaning literally a 'seer'.

The most prestigous title of was *druis* (from an original *dru-wid-is, meaning 'strong-knowledge-possessor'). These druids were entrusted with arbitration in both individual and public disputes, and were thought to mediate between their societies and the mysterious powers of destiny, being 'learned in the divine nature and, so to say, familiar with it'. In other words, they inherited the shamanic function from a more primitive stage of culture. It is difficult to speculate on the stages by which the rather spontaneous office of a mediator with the spirit world developed into a more formalised learned figure, but all indications are that by the 5th or 4th Centuries BC the druids had some form of standardised training and systematic dogma while still retaining the aura of mystery.

That these practitioners of the sacred had a strong role in political matters is evident from many Classical accounts. The Celts are described as being much given to superstition, which would entail among other things the attribution of supernatural powers to the druidic class. Thus we read that they carefully obeyed the druids and poets, and that these men had influence not only over friends but over enemies as well. 'For oftentimes, as armies approach each other in line of battle with their swords drawn and their spears raised for the charge, these men come forth between them and stop the conflict, as though they had spellbound some kinds of wild animals'. This is surely a dramatised version of the situation, but it is clear from the sentiment that rhetorics, sacredly pronounced by their druids and seers, were generally understood to have magical power.

The Classical authors claim that the Celts were hot-tempered and very jealous of their honour, and it would be natural for them to consider the social and spiritual realms as reflecting each other. Thus, it is no surprise to read

Posidonius's comment that 'the Celts have in their company, in war as well as in peace, companions whom they call parasites. These men pronounce their praises before the whole assembly, and before each of the chieftains in turn as they listen. Their entertainers are called bards—these are poets who deliver eulogies in song'. Using information from the same Posidonius, another writer states that the the bards of the Celts sing 'sometimes an eulogy and sometimes a satire'. Such references accord well with the ancient belief among European peoples that praise uttered by a poet or rhetorician has a salutory effect on its subject, whereas satire has a destructive effect. This belief seems to have survived with particular vigour among the Celts, whom the same writer accuses of being 'boasters and threateners and given to self-dramatisation'.

By the end of the 5th Century BC, the Celts had reasons to be boastful. They had established themselves firmly as far as the Atlantic in the west, and had also reached the sea-coast in the north and were settling in the adjacent parts of Britain, where they were quickly making themselves dominant over the indigenous inhabitants. At the other end of their territory, groups of them had been crossing the Pyrenees for generations and penetrating into the Iberian Peninsula. Esconced in strong hill-forts, these continued to exert pressure on ancient non-Indo-European peoples of the Peninsula such as the Iberians, the Tartessians, and the Basques. As a result a new mixed population, called Celtiberi, was becoming the dominant force in all of north-east and central Spain, and in other scattered areas beyond. About the same time Celts began to establish settlements on the south-eastern slopes of the Alps. It is accepted that this great expansion was directly due to an explosion in their population.

As a group, admittedly a rather diffuse one, they were reaching the climax of their strength, but the German tribes proved a sturdy barrier to their spread directly northwards across the Rhine, and eastern expansion was impossible due to the spheres of influence there of powerful peoples such as the Scythians, the Thracians, and the Greeks. Tempted by the fertile plains of Italy, and feeling the impulse for a new and massive thrust, they decided to move south.

Modern illustration of the body of a British Celtic chieftain borne on a litter to burial by nobles. Tribesmen follow the procession, which is led by druids. The body would be cremated, and the ashes placed in an urn, over which a tumulus would be raised. (From a painting by W W Collins.)

Chapter 2

THE CELTS IN ITALY

From the beginning of the 4th Century BC, droves of Celts began to cross the Alps and descend into the Valley of the Po, in Italy. The Classical writers give as reason for these invasions a desire to possess the riches of Italy, in particular the wine, for which the Celts had acquired a strong taste. Pliny gives a rather symbolic setting to this when he tells a story of how a skilled Celtic craftsman named Helico had sojourned for a while in Rome and, on his return home, whetted the appetites of his fellows with 'some dried figs and grapes and some samples of oil and wine'. This caused them to wish to possess such fine food even by means of war if necessary. Such an anecdote was, of course, an over-simplification of the motives of what these writers regarded as a foreign and rather strange race.

Livy, while also claiming that the Celts were attracted south by 'the delicious fruits and especially the wine', gives an even more personal reason for these initial Celtic incursions. It concerns a nobleman of the Etruscan city of Clusium (now Chiusi), called Arruns, whose wife had been seduced by his protegé, a young man of powerful connections on whom it was difficult to gain revenge. To attain his purpose, therefore, Arruns decided to seek help from the Celts, and sent wine to them in order to entice them to cross the Alps and attack Clusium.

Whatever was the nature of the contacts between the Celts and this Arruns, a change in the political balance of the area would have been a more rational cause, and a more realistic temptation for the Celts. In reality, the power of the Etruscans, who had dominated the area for centuries, was in decline, and this would have tempted foreign adventurers. Celtic influences on some of the peoples of northern Italy can be discerned in the archaeological record for some time previously, so it is clear that those groups who began to cross the Alps in large numbers already had good knowledge of the areas into which they were descending.

As the nation nearest to the Celts on their south-eastern flank, the Illyrians had borne the brunt of Celtic ambitions for some time, and a vignette illustrating Celtic guile in their early dealings with them is given by the Greek writer Theopompus. Being aware of the Illyrians' taste for fine food, the Celts 'prepared a very sumptuous banquet in their tents for all the soldiers, and mixed with the food an herb of intoxicating properties which strongly purged their bowels'. It would appear that the Celts prepared this feast in their own encampment, and then allowed the Illyrians to seize the camp and partake of it. The result, at any rate, was dramatic, for Theopompus states that, while in this helpless state, many of the Illyrians were captured and slain by the Celts, while others 'unable to endure the workings of their stomachs, threw themselves into the rivers'.

This account is no doubt embellished, but it is at any rate clear that the Celts were encroaching on territories to the south of them for some time before the 4th Century BC. It is obvious, also, that the cause of such a desire for conquest was a population explosion which had occurred in the country of the Celts north of the Alps, causing discord and dissension among them. As we have seen in Chapter 1, the archaeological evidence shows that the Celts had been divided into fairly distinct kingdoms for several centuries. By the time of the invasions of northern Italy, names appear for some of these particular population-groups, and in particular for those who were spreading south.

That tribes in their entirety were not involved in the great movements is obvious from the fact that those with similar group-names continued to inhabit the areas north of the Alps.

Part of a horse's harness found at Manerbio, Brescia, in Italy, believed to be Cenomani Celt territory in about the 1st Century BC. Measuring about 4in (10cm) in diameter, it is made from silver and is engraved with a triskele surrounded by 20 heads with stiff hair and moustaches. Now at Museo Civico Romano.

What actually happened was that sections of these groups, finding living-room more difficult in their native areas, decided to risk their fortunes further afield. Another reason advanced for the spread of the Celts is transhumance, the custom of seeking summer habitations in areas away from the homeland. One Latin source, using Celtic tradition, likens such movements to a ver sacrum, a religious festival observed by the Romans in spring. As the Etruscan power declined, leaving the other Italic and Illyrian peoples of the area without the necessary defence to withstand large-scale Celtic influxes, such periodic migrations would have grown bolder, eventually developing into permanent and uncontested settlements.

The first of the invasion forces to arrive were a large group of the Insubres – who belonged to the powerful Aedui people– and they were followed by sections of other tribes, such as the Senones and the Boii. These had reputedly been encouraged to depart their patrimony by Ambicatus, king of the Bituriges, who was the most powerful figure among the Celts north of the Alps. His name attests to a thirst for power and an ambition for conquest, for it meant 'he who turns battles'. The designation Bituriges must have originated in a royal title— its singular Biturix (meaning 'world-king')—and we can therefore assume that the tribe had developed their identity from a role of supremacy among their fellow-Celts. Ambicatus may not in fact have been a historical person, but rather a traditional symbol of their kingship cultivated by the Bituriges.

In the late 5th Century BC, the Bituriges held the kingship over a confederacy of Celts, which included the Arverni, Boii, Aedui, Aulerci, Andes, Lingones, and Senones. The leading position attributed to Ambicatus among the Celts of his time must accordingly have been in large measure due to the ability of the Bituriges tribe to make war. The legend of Ambicatus reached the ears of the Romans, for Livy describes him as a rich and courageous ruler and states that during his reign there were extremely abundant harvests. This must be an echo of an ancient Celtic belief that prosperity attended the rule of a good king who embodied the ritual quality of 'truth'. It is therefore obvious that, in his search for the reasons for the Celtic expansion of the early 4th Century BC, Livy decided to make use of mythical history as preserved by the Celts themselves.

In his account, Livy states that the population grew so rapidly that, by the time that Ambicatus was an old man, he decided to instruct some of his people to relieve the strain of overcrowding by seeking new settlements far away. His sister had two very enterprising sons, called Bellovesus and Segovesus, and these two were sent to 'settle in whatever locality which the gods should by augury assign to them'. Thus this major migration was understood as a ritualised act. Notwithstanding the family connection claimed for them with a legendary king, the two leaders may well have been historical characters. Their names may accordingly have been prestigious titles conferred on them either in their own lifetime or posthumously. *Bellovesus* meant 'the Slayer' and *Segovesus* meant 'the Victor'. We read that the gods preferred that Segovesus should move with his followers into the Hercynian forest to the north (the Black Forest and Bohemia), whereas to Bellovesus was allotted the more promising prospect of Italy. Most of Bellovesus's followers would appear to have been Insubres, but Livy claims that he also had surplus groups from the Bituriges, Arverni, Senones, Ambarri, Carnutes, and Aulerci.

BELLOVESUS CROSSES THE ALPS

On reaching the Alps with 'an enormous force of horse and foot', he hestitated to survey the mountains and decide on a way through. While thus engaged, Livy claims that news came that the Greeks from Marseilles were being attacked by enemies, and that Bellovesus went to their assistance. This probably reflects an attack from neighbouring Celtic people on Marseilles, and how the Greeks of that colony were in a position to summon the help of other Celts. It would appear that Bellovesus had some such defence-pact with the Massilians, and that they in turn assisted him and his followers to find a way across the Alps. This is a strong indication that they crossed from that western side.

Livy, in fact, has them going through the passes of Taurine and the valley of Duria. They defeated an Etruscan tribe, the Tuscani, in a battle at Ticino, and Livy states that, on finding that the name Insubres had already been attached to the surrounding countryside, they took this as a good omen and founded a settlement there, which they called Mediolanum (literally 'middle plain', now Milan). The likelihood here is that some of the Insubres had earlier become mixed, perhaps through trade-contacts, with the indigenous inhabitants, speakers of the Lepontic language which was closely related to Celtic. These Lepontic people had only recently been subjected by the Etruscans, and the name of the Insubres would therefore have been well-known in the area.

Soon after, a group of Cenomani (who were a branch of the Aulerci) crossed by the same pass, under a leader called Elitovius. This incursion was welcomed by the Insubres leader Bellovesus, and they founded settlements in the neighbourhood of Brescia and Verona. Others still followed, but the next major incursion was that of the Boii and Lingones. Finding all the country occupied by their fellow Celts, they crossed the Po on rafts and drove the Etruscans and Umbrians before them as far as the Appennine mountains. Finally, the Senones descended on Italy and, passing by the other Celtic settlements, pushed as far along the coast as Ancona. These invaders did not break the power of the Etruscans completely, but instead made large settlements which the Etruscans were unable to eject from their territory. The Veneti people in north-east Italy (around present-day Venice) must have been considered too strong to meddle with, for the Celtic invaders by-passed them on their way south.

Polybius, who wrote a century earlier than Livy, also has the Celts first entering from the north-west. He claims that the Laevi and Libici were the first of these tribes to settle on the

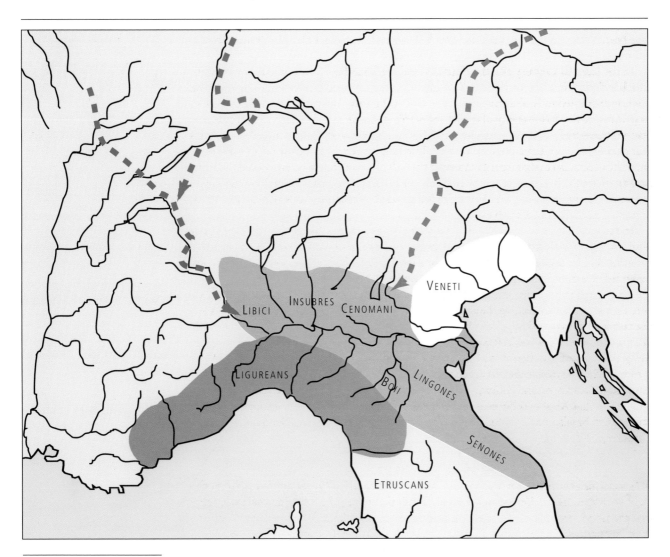

The descent on Italy by the Celtic invaders, and the areas occupied by them. Indigenous peoples were pushed aside by them , such as the Ligureans to the west and the Etrucsans to the south. Scattered groups of both Ligureans and Etruscans seem, however, to have continued to live within areas taken over by the newcomers.
The Veneti, a strong indigenous people in the north-east, were largely untouched.

southern side of the Alps. They occupied the area near the source of the Po, which would have been adjacent to the strip of land held by the Greeks of Marseilles. After them, states Polybius, came 'the largest tribe of all', the Insubres; and then the Cenomani, who moved south along the bank of the river. Further south, in the Appennine district, the Anares settled, and to the east of them the Boii. These Boii and other tribes, such as the Lingones and Senones, must have crossed the Alps at a more eastern point, such as the Brenner or St Gothard Passes. Polybius agrees that the Lingones settled on the Adriatic, and that the Senones went even further south along that coastline. He gives an interesting description of the way of life of the intruders:

> *They lived in open villages, without any permanent buildings. As they made their bed of straw or leaves, and fed on meat, and followed no pursuits but those of war and agriculture, they lived simple lives without being acquainted with any science or art whatever. Each man's property, moreover, consisted in cattle and gold; as they were the only things that could easily be carried with them, when they from place to place, and changed their dwellings as fancy directed. They put a high esteem, however, on friendship: for the man who had the largest number of clients or companions in his wanderings was looked upon as the most formidable and powerful member of the tribe. In the early days of their settlement, they did not merely subdue the territory which they occupied, but rendered also many of the neighbouring peoples subject to them, overawing them by their audacity.*

Within the first decade of the 4th Century BC, then, Celtic tribes had spread their dominance over most of the countryside between the Alps and the Appennines, a region which was afterwards known to the Romans as Cisalpine Gaul. Such a rapid change in the power structure of so large an area could hardly be expected to bring stability. Thus, when the

Senones in the year 391 BC began to threaten the Etruscan city of Clusium (now Chiusi, on the southern side of the Appennines) a chain of events began which would bring the Celts into confrontation with the emerging super-power in central Italy, the city of Rome.

The inhabitants of Clusium had refused to give support to their fellow Etruscans, the Veii, in a recent war with the Romans, and now in their hour of need they looked for repayment of the debt from the Romans. A delegation sent by them to the Roman Senate was refused immediate military support, but three sons of Fabius Ambustus were sent as ambassadors to the Senones. The Romans intended to secure the Senones as allies, but their ambassadors made it clear that the armed force of Rome would be available if Clusium were attacked. Somewhat angered by this, the Senones replied that they would keep the peace only if the Clusines ceded some territory to them. If this were refused, they said, 'we shall fight, while you are still here, so that you may report to those at home how far the Celts surpass all other men in courage!'

The Roman ambassadors chided the Senones, demanding to know what right the invaders had in the area, and the Senones replied that they carried their right in their weapons, and that 'everything belonged to the brave'. The meeting broke up, and both sides prepared for battle. When battle was joined, the Roman ambassadors exceded their function by participating on the side of the Clusines. During the fighting, a Celtic chief charged right at the Etruscan standards. Seeing this, one of the ambassadors ran his spear through the Celt, slew him, and was in the act of despoiling his body when he was recognised by the other Celts. Shocked by this intervention, the Celts withdrew in sullen anger, uttering threats against the Romans. Some were in favour of an immediate advance on Rome, but the older men persuaded them to send a complaint to the Senate instead. No satisfaction was given and, instead of being repimanded, the Roman ambassadors were actually honoured by the Senate for the role they had played.

Celtic hordes, under the leadership of Brennos, advance southwards towards Rome. A woodcut imaginatively depicting the scene, from W Wägner, Rom. Bd. 1 (O Spamer: Leipzig, 1862) Coll. Archiv für Kunst and Geschichte, Berlin.

The Celts took this as a prelude to outright war, and undoubtedly the Senones were reinforced at this time by strong contingents from the other tribes in Cisalpine Gaul. Some time must have been spent in making preparations for the impending war, but Livy prefers to imagine the gathering Celtic forces as acting out of impetuosity. He claims that 'as a nation they cannot control their passions' and so, burning with rage, they seized their standards and a massive army of them set out without delay for Rome. 'Horses and men, spread far and wide, covered an immense tract of country - wherever they went they made it understood by loud shouts that they were going to Rome.' In 388 BC, they met the Roman army about 11 miles (7km) from the city, where the Allia river flows into the Tiber. Livy states that 'their hideous howls and discordant clamour filled everything with dreadful noise'. Their leader was one Brennos and he, very astutely, attacked the Roman reserves first, and when these broke before his charge the whole Roman force was seized with panic and took to flight.

Astonished at this easy victory, and fearing a ruse, the Celts did not immediately follow the fleeing Romans, but soon began to despoil the dead and, as was their custom, 'to pile up the arms in heaps'. They then resumed their march on Rome, which they reached before sunset and found the gates open and no force protecting the city. The Roman soldiers who had got safely home made frantic preparations to defend the hill of the Capitol, while all night long the cautious Celts circled around the walls of the city uttering wild war-cries. As morning dawned on July 18 of the year 388, the Celtic army entered the city, and found the aging patricians sitting in their full regalia. A Celtic soldier, half in jest and half with wonder, began to stroke the beard of one of these patricians, and was immediately struck on the head by the old man with his ivory staff. The Celts in fury then slaughtered all the patricians and set to burning parts of the city.

After several days of burning and plunder, they decided to make an assault on the remaining Roman forces in the Capitol. Raising their battle-cries and locking their shields together over their heads, they advanced to the attack, but the Romans rushed on them from the top of the hill and drove them back down. The Celts then decided on a blockade, but this delay allowed the Romans who had fled to Veii to re-assemble, and these were joined by other support groups from other parts of Latium. Under the leadership of their skilled general, Camillus, they renewed the war, attacking foraging parties of Celts and threatening to relieve the siege. Another attempt by the Celts to take the Capitol failed—according to legend this was under cover of darkness, but the sacred geese warned the Roman defenders and the attack was again repulsed. Livy states that famine and malaria then began to play havoc with the Celtic army, unaccustomed to prolonged fighting in so warm a climate, so that in the end they had to pile the bodies of their dead in heaps and burn them indiscriminately at a place which became known as the *Busta Gallica* ('the Celtic Pyres').

Feeling all this increasing pressure, coming so quickly upon their initial successes, the Celts were disheartened and agreed to a parley. Their leader

Brennos measuring the gold tribute from the Romans. Later writers claimed that the Celtic leader had tricked and insulted the Romans, but this may have been invented to discredit the Celts, whom the Romans never forgave for overcoming them on this occasion.

Brennos met with the Roman tribune Quintus Sulpicius, and a ransom of one thousand pounds of gold was agreed to be paid by the Romans. Livy claims that the Celts were despicably mean in this discussion and that they tried to cheat at the weighing of the gold. When the tribune protested, Brennos threw his sword into the scale, exclaiming: 'Woe to the vanquished!' He then agreed to withdraw from Rome and its immediate area, a miscalculation which would have disastrous effects on the Celtic peoples in the long haul of history.

The ancient historians reckoned the number of Celtic warriors engaged in the battle of the Allia at 30,000 men, and this gives an indication of the magnitude of their settlements in the north of Italy. We can surmise that the total population of all the tribes together, including women and children, amounted to hundreds of thousands. Such a large number could not easily be driven back across the Alps, and their settlements soon mingled with and took over towns such as Brixia, Bergamo, Como, Modena, Bologna and Trent, the latter two of which get their names from the Celtic *Bononia* and *Tridentum*. The native peoples of this area of Cisalpine Gaul, such as the Ligurians, Etruscans and Umbrians, survived alongside the newcomers, in some areas being subjected by them, in others sharing the countryside in uneasy accommodations between the communities.

After their advance was stopped at Rome, however, the Celts fell into difficulties of their own making. More of their people were crossing the Alps, mostly reinforcements for their armies in Italy, and it became increasingly difficult to facilitate these mercenaries with land and wealth. Polybius states that the Celts in Italy were being harassed by their cousins on the northern side of the Alps, who were 'comparing their own barren districts with the rich land

Titus Manlius overcoming a giant Celtic warrior in single combat on the bridge over the Anio, as the two armies look on. The scene imaginatively portrayed on a copper engraving by Matthäus Merion (1593-1650). From Johann Ludwig Gottfried, Historische Chronica *(Frankfurt) – Coll. Archiv fur Kunst und Geschgichte, Berlin.*

occupied by the others'. Such internal tension no doubt contributed in large measure to the fact that the Celts in general did not follow up their advantage against the weakened Romans. They continued to carry out sporadic raids, some well south of Rome, but did not renew their assault in a comprehensive way for a generation or so.

The Romans had some respite and time to reorganise until in or about the year 367 BC, when the Celts carried out a large raid as far south as Alba in Latium and plundered the area. Six years later, the Celts were back again, encamping in a large force on the river Anio and threatening Rome. The Roman dictator Titus Quinctius marched out of the city with a large army, and camped on the opposite side of the river. Then a single Celt of enormous size, in multicoloured dress and painted armour inlaid with gold, came to the bridge over the Anio and shouted out a challenge to the bravest man in Rome to fight him in single combat. A young Roman nobleman called Titus Manlius volunteered to take up the challenge. On seeing a much smaller man than himself come forward, the Celt stuck out his tongue in mockery. When they came to close quarters, the Celt slashed at Manlius with his great sword, but to no effect, and the Roman stabbed at him with his shorter sword and slew him. He seized the torque from the corpse of the Celt and put it on his own neck, thus earning the nickname 'Torquatus'. The whole Celtic army was much disheartened by this, and next night they left their camp and withdrew to Campania.

Forging an alliance with the Tiburtines, the Celts continued the war until the following year, 360 BC, when they were defeated within sight of Rome itself by a new dictator, Quintus Servilius Ahala. The Celtic survivors fled to the city of Tibur, where they were welcomed and given refuge, while the Romans were too occupied with their struggles against other Italic peoples to pursue their advantage. Again, in 358 BC, a Gaulish force advanced as far as Praeneste, but were repulsed by a Roman army under Gaius Sulpicius. They were driven with great slaughter into the mountains and woods, and Livy claims that the Romans collected from their spoils a considerable quantity of gold.

A much larger incursion into Roman territory occurred seven years later, and near Alba the Celts were encountered by a strong Roman army which occupied the higher ground.

A Roman relief (in France) of a legionary fighting a Celtic warrior. Note the Roman's helmet and the bare head of the Celt.

Attacking 'with wild shouts', the Celts tried to charge uphill in the face of a torrent of javelins and spears, but their charge was broken. Thinking they had already gained victory, the Romans descended to the plain, but were confronted by a fresh troop of Celtic warriors. Here the Romans showed their superior tactical skill, and Livy says that the Celts broke ranks 'for lack of proper command or leadership', and retreated in total disarray to the distant hills.

Yet again, in the winter of 349-348 BC, the Celts came down from the Appennine heights, being unable to withstand the severity of the winter weather', and – without much regard for strategy – fought an indecisive battle with Greek pirates who were ravaging the coast off Rome. Eventually, they were encountered by a Roman army of nearly 40,000 men under Camillus, son of the famous general. Realising that the Celts lived off plunder, Camillus embarked on a policy of preventing individual raids rather than engaging in all-out confrontation. For the purpose of controlling the whole area against such sudden attacks, he set up a large camp as headquarters in the Pomptine district.

Livy cannot refrain from telling another dramatic anecdote here. He relates how a huge and heavily armed Celt approached the Roman camp, demanded silence by striking his shield with his spear, and then through an interpreter issued a challenge to single combat. A young tribune called Marcus Valerius took the field. As he faced the Celtic warrior, a raven suddenly alighted on the helmet of Valerius, and joined with its beak and claws in the attack on the Celt. Bewildered and half-blinded, the warrior was slain by Valerius, and the raven then flew off towards the east. Both sides took this as a sign of divine intervention on behalf of the Romans, who proceeded to attack the Celts when the latter went to recover their fallen warrior. This, we read, developed into a general melée, and then into an outright battle, from which the Celts turned and fled towards Apulia and the sea. Camillus is quoted as shouting to his men to 'cut down the Gaulish hordes around their fallen leader!'

These stories of single combat offered by the Celts before a battle require some investigation. First of all, the context in which the stories are proffered by Livy is not entirely reliable. It is clear that the Celts did not succeed in defeating the Roman armies during the two decades described by Livy, but the author himself admits that raiding for plunder rather than war for conquest was their purpose. We can accept that several of such raids were repulsed by the Romans, but others must have been largely successful. Indeed, regarding the events of the year 349-348 BC, instead of the great Roman victory in the dual battle described by Livy, Polybius states that the Romans got intelligence of an advance by 'a great force' of Celts and,

Battle scene on a cinerary urn from Chiusi, Sicily, dating to the 3rd or 2nd Century BC. The naked warriors would appear to have been Celts.

mustering their allies, they marched forth in eagerness to fight a decisive battle. 'But the Galatae were dismayed at their approach, and besides weakened by internal feuds, retreated homewards as soon as night fell, with all the appearance of a regular flight.' In other words, the Celts were too cautious to risk a disastrous defeat, and were shrewd enough to see that there was no great plunder to be had on that occasion.

Given this, one is prepared to doubt the veracity of the all-conquering ability of the Romans in that century, and even more so to doubt the inevitable victory of Roman champions in single combat. The nickname Torquatus given to Manlius and his descendants points to some episode which had him overcome a well-caparisoned Celtic warrior and seizing the torcus from his neck, but the circumstances of that individual struggle need not have been as symbolic as presented by Livy. One thing is clear from both Classical and native Celtic sources—that the Celts had a custom, when two armies were drawn up in opposition to each area, for a champion from either side to engage in single combat as a prelude to the general battle. Diodorus Siculus, for instance, drew the following description of Celtic battle-custom from the work of Posidonius: 'When the armies are drawn up in battle-array they are wont to advance before the battle-line and to challenge the bravest of their opponent to single combat, at the same time brandishing before them their arms so as to terrify their foe. And, when someone accepts their challenge to battle, they loudly recite the deeds of valour of their ancestors and proclaim their own valorous quality, at the same time abusing and making little of their opponent and generally attempting to rob him beforehand of his fighting spirit.' This was the type of Celtic practice of which Livy had heard, and which he or his sources turned to the propaganda advantage of the Romans.

The episode of the crow must spring from a similar Celtic tradition. The raven or carrion-crow—which haunts the battlefield waiting to prey on the carnage—had long been a symbol of war for the Celts, and indeed such a bird was represented on helmets of some of their leading warriors for a long time. The image was assimilated to that of the war-goddess, which was

Marcus Valerius overcoming a Celtic warrior in single combat. The raven assists Valerius, as the two armies advance towards each other. The arms and armour are inaccurately depicted in this 17th Cntury copper engraving by Matthäus Merion. From Johann Ludwig Gottfried, Historische Chronica *(Frankfurt) – Coll. Archiov fur Kunst und Geschichte, Berlin.*

the form taken by the land-goddess on behalf of her adherents in time of strife. She was known as Catubodua ('battle-raveness'), a designation which survived with the very same meaning in Irish tradition as *cathbhadhbh* or *badhbh chatha*. Livy's claim that Celtic armies were demoralised by defeat of their champions in single combat accords with the order which he attributes to the younger Camillus to cut down the Gauls 'around their fallen leader'. This also rings true to Celtic tradition, for Irish sources state that 'battle is discontinued after the loss of a lord'.

Two major failings of Celtic armies are accurately pinpointed by Livy: their lack of over-all planning, and their quarrelsomeness and disunity. Polybius agrees with this, for—in describing the situation at the beginning of the 3rd Century BC — he shows how their internal tensions and their short-sightedness caused increasing problems for them. He relates how the Celts in Italy were alarmed by a threatening movement of the Transalpine tribes, and tried to divert a new invading horde by presents and by appeals to their ties of kindred. Eventually, they had no alternative but to recommend a new attack on Rome, which would allow the newcomers full

Face of Celtic warrior in Italy from contemporaneous silver engraving. See also photos on page 25 and opposite.

Silver Celtic shield with profile details, from Manerbio, near Brescia, in the territory of the Cenomani. Now displayed in Civico Musei d'Arte e Storia, Brescia, Italy.

scope for their enthusiasm, and the Cisalpine Celts themselves offered to join in the expedition. They furthermore enlisted the support of an Etruscan army, and in the resulting raid on Roman territories in 299 BC they took a great quantity of booty. 'But when they got home, they quarrelled over the division of the spoil, and in the end destroyed most of it, as well as the best of their own force. This is the way of the Galatae when they have appropriated their neighbours' property, and it mostly arises from brutish drunkenness and intemperate feeling.'

A logical strategy for the Celts in these wars would have been to forge close military links with the other peoples of northern and central Italy whose interests were being threatened by the Romans. They were very slow to realise the wisdom of this, however, and in the year 296 BC joined a combined force of Etruscans, Samnites, and Umbrians only after much coaxing by the others. The Romans were alarmed at this development for – as Livy says – the Celts were 'a race born to the clash of arms, fierce not only by nature but moreover by their hatred of the Roman people' and 'what was most dreaded at Rome was a Gaulish rising'. They had good reason for this fear, for in the following year the Senones surrounded and wiped out a whole legion at Clusium. The Roman consuls, Fabius and Decius, who were hastening to that place, got the first inkling of what had happened when they caught sight of Celtic horsemen 'carrying heads on their horses' breasts and fixed on their spears, singing their usual song of triumph'.

The plan was to destroy all the Roman legions by a combined force of Celts and Samnites taking the field against the advancing Romans, while the Etruscans and Umbrians were to attack the large Roman base-camp at Sentinum. Three traitors from the combined camp at Clusium, however, kept the Romans informed of all plans, and the Romans decided to draw the attention of the Etruscans and Umbrians away by ravaging their lands. A large force undertook this work of destruction, and these two Celtic forces had no alternative but to go and defend their people. Then the Romans pressed the combined force of Celts and Samnites into a confrontation near Clusium. As the opposing armies drew up to face each other, Livy relates that a wolf chased a hind down from the mountains and onto the plain between them. The hind raced towards the Gauls, but the surprised wolf headed for the Roman lines, where it was let through with great acclamation. They took this as a portent, for the wolf was sacred to Mars, the Roman god of war.

The numbers on both sides were enormous. Livy mentions as an exaggeration a report that the combined Celts and Samnites had over half a million infantry, with 46,000 cavalry and 1,000 chariots, but even a third of such a force would have been massive. The Romans had four full legions. The Gauls were on the right wing of their side, and the Samnites on the left, and Livy remarks that if the Etruscan army had been there it would have meant certain defeat for the Romans. As it was, the fighting was ferocious, lasting all day long without any advantage to either side. The Roman commander Fabius decided to remain on the defensive and to hold his lines for as long as possible, knowing that the Celts were very fierce and determined on their first onslaught but tended to tire and to succumb to the heat as time wore on. The other commander, Decius, however, was more impetuous, and he launched his cavalry with full vigour onto the Celtic lines. They broke through the Celtic cavalry and set upon the infantry, but suddenly they were alarmed by a style of fighting which they had never before encountered. The Celts, standing up in their chariots, and hurling their weapons, bore down on them with a fearful clamour of hooves and wheels.

The cavalry of Decius was seized with panic and fled through the lines of their own infantry. Then the Celts came at them, wreaking havoc in all directions. The Roman commander Decius realised that he had almost lost the battle and, solemnly dedicating himself to the gods, rode his horse right into the Celtic mass, where he was cut down. The Celts crowded exultantly around his body, flinging their javelins in all directions 'as if they had lost their wits'.

The patient and resourceful Fabius, however, was determined to turn disaster into victory. Perceiving that the madness of war was upon the Celts, he sent reinforcements over to the weakened Roman flank, encouraging them to renew the attack. The Celts stood in close formation with their shields overlapping in front of them, and the slaughter continued there in stalemate. Meanwhile, Fabius pushed the Samnites over towards their Celtic allies and, judging that his opponents were beginning to show signs of fatigue, he collected all his reserve troops, chased the Samnites through the Celtic lines, and then ordered a new attack on the rear of the Celts.

Eventually the Celtic formation broke, and the Romans had prevailed. The Celts and Samnites lost 25,000 dead and 8,000 captured, while Roman losses totalled nearly 8,000. It took the Romans a long time to locate the body of the consul Decius, for he had been buried under a mound of Celtic corpses.

ROMANS SET UP FIRST COLONY IN CELTIC LANDS

That many of the defeated forces got away, however, is clear from what Polybius has to say about this battle. The Romans, having killed a large number of Celts and Samnites, 'forced the survivors to retreat in hot haste, each to his own land'. The Samnites were able to continue the war for several years more; and, as for the Celts, within ten years they were besieging the town of Arretium (now Arezzo). Polybius describes how the Romans went to the assistance of the town 'and were beaten in an engagement under its walls'. The Roman praetor Lucius was killed in this battle and many Roman prisoners were taken. The new Roman praetor Manlius Curius felt constrained to send ambassadors to the Celts to treat for the prisoners, but the ambasadors were murdered – perhaps in recollection of the treachery of Roman ambassadors to the Celts a century before. The furious Romans then sent another army to the area, and in a pitched battle in 283 BC they cut the army of the Senones to pieces. The rest of the Senones were then expelled from most of their territory, and Roman colonies were planted at Sena Gallica, north of Ancona, and further north still at Ariminum (now Rimini) – the first ever in Celtic lands. The Romans boasted that their Consul, Livius Drusus, recovered from the Senones the thousand pounds of gold which had been paid in ransom of Rome itself a hundred years before.

Frightened by these events, the other frontline Celtic people, the Boii, called up their men, made an alliance with the Etruscans, and gave battle to the Romans near the small lake of Vadimo, close to the Tiber between Volsinii and Falerii. The Etruscans lost half of their army there, while scarcely any of the Boii army escaped. As a result, the Boii were facing extinction in the area, and in the following year, 282 BC, found it necessary to enlist all of their young men who had just come of age in order to withstand the Romans, But they were defeated again, and had to surrender and accept Roman settlements on their lands. For a whole generation and more, the Celts of Cisalpine Gaul had no choice but to accept Roman dictates and continuing evictions.

The tidal-wave of expansion into Italy had been in surge for over a century, but it had finally been turned and, instead of the Celts making encroachments into Roman territory, it was the Romans who were beginning to encroach on the hard-won soil of the Po Valley. Italy had proved, and would further prove, to be a precarious adventure for the Celts, but it was not the only stage for their ambitions. Territories much further away from the homeland were also beckoning and, at this time, Celtic warriors were making dramatic progress in these.

Celtic warrior with loot, from a sculpture of the 2nd Century BC (height 17.72in/45cm). Detail from a terracotta frieze in a temple at Civita Alba, near Sassoferrato, Italy. This bordered on the territory of the Senones. Now at Museo Civico, Bologna.

Chapter 3

THE THRUST TO THE EAST

hen—according to tradition—Ambicatus, the celebrated king of the Bituriges, directed his nephews to carve out new territories for themselves and their followers, the area of the Hercynian forest was assigned to Segovesus. This great ancient forest stretched eastwards from the Celtic territories in southern Germany and Switzerland, and was less attractive to invaders than the Italian plains which had been assigned to Bellovesus. Nevertheless, Segovesus proved also to be a daunting warrior and a shrewd leader, and he made rapid progress with his host of warriors. This great movement would appear to have included substantial groups from the Boii (originally Bogii, 'strikers'), and particularly from the Volcae (literally 'wolves', meaning raiding warriors). A section of these Volcae came to be known as Tectosages (Celtic Textosages, meaning 'migrants in search of wealth'). One ancient author dramatises the adventure by claiming that Segovesus and his followers were 'guided by birds, for the Celts are pre-eminent in the art of augury'.

It is probable that Segovesus and his followers were indeed reassured at the start of their expedition by signs and prophecies. The undertaking, at any rate, proved very successful. The powerful Illyrians and the Pannonians stood in the way but failed to prevent them. Advancing along the Danube, they reached eastern Austria, Hungary, and the northern Balkans within a few years and established themselves strongly in these areas. Unfortunately we know little about the actual career of Segovesus himself, but we do know that he and his immediate descendants benefited from instability in that whole eastern area. The Illyrians were at war with the Macedonians, a factor which left their western flank quite vulnerable to Celtic expansion.

In the year 393 BC the Illyrians forced the Macedonians to pay them tribute, and in 359 they slew the Macedonian king Perdiccas in battle. Before they could devote their attention to the Celtic intruders, however, the Macedonians recovered and, under the leadership of Perdiccas's brother Philip drove the Illyrians from their territory. After many successes, Philip was assassinated in 336 BC by one of his bodyguard. The assassin was a Macedonian, but the weapon used was a Celtic dagger. The accession to power in 335 of Philip's son, Alexander the Great, sounded a death-knell for the Illyrian empire. While Alexander was embarking on his campaign against the Thracians in the area of the eastern Danube, the Celts felt themselves ready for further incursions into the territory of the Illyrians and Pannonians. It was at this time that their ambassadors appeared at the court of Alexander, impressing him with their brashness and securing an alliance of friendship with him. Thus was formalised a convergence of interest which had existed for some time, and a situation which aptly suited the ambitions of the Celts.

These Celts are reported to have settled along the Ionian Gulf, which shows that they had progressed southwards by the flank of the strong Veneti and had taken over part of modern Slovenia. To go further at that time would have incurred the hostility of Alexander, but after his death in the year 323 BC they were once more on the move. In the year 310, under the leadership of Molistomos, they drove the Illyrians before them, and the Macedonian leader Cassander felt obliged to intervene and take the Illyrians under his protection. This, however, had little effect on Celtic ambitions, who within some years had reached as far as Bulgaria.

Alexander the Great (355-323 BC), Macedonian Emperor who was a bulwark against Celtic expansion into the Balkans and with whom they came to terms. From the Issus mosaic, c 100 BC.

There, in 298 a large body of them clashed with Cassander's army on the slopes of Mount Haemos. Cassander triumphed, but further afield the Celts were still advancing, and a second large body—under the leadership of Cambaules—marched on Thrace. The power of the Thracians had been reduced by the Macedonians, and now much of the area fell into Celtic hands. A contemporary Greek writer described how the terror of the Celtic name was so great that 'kings, even before they were attacked, bought peace with large sums of money'. Finally, weakened by divisions and internal fighting over the succession to Cassander, Macedonia itself came under threat.

The followers of Cambaules, flushed with victory and greedy for more booty, decided to try their luck further. At their continual instigation, a great force of warriors—both on foot and mounted — assembled and, after some deliberation, their leaders decided to divide into three sections. Thus, in the year 281 BC, three armies of Celts moved southwards to attack the

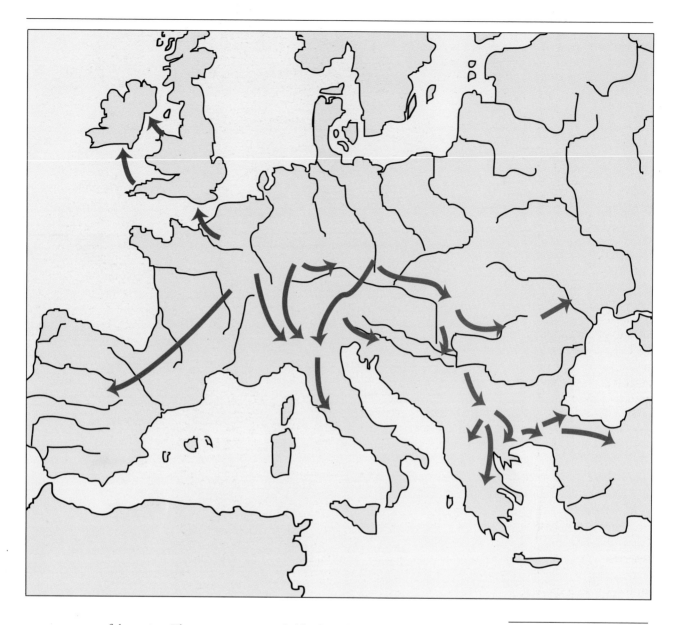

greatest power of the region. The eastern army was led by Cerethrios, and was to attack the Thracians and the Triballi. The central army was under the dual command of Brennos and Acichorios, and was to attack Paeonia. The western army, led by a chieftain who is known to us by the nickname Bolgios, had the most daunting task, that of attacking the Macedonians and their new Illyrian allies. This campaign threatened to make the Celts the most powerful people in all the Balkan Peninsula.

The advance of Bolgios was towards the territory ruled by Ptolemy, the Macedonian king. This Ptolemy was notorious for his treachery and cruelty, and had been only a year and a half in the kingship after a chequered career. When his earlier intrigues in Egypt failed, he had fled to the Syrian court, where he was given refuge and protection by King Seleucus 1. Seleucus was one of the Alexander's generals, who after the death of the great leader had fought each other for different parts of his empire, and, by a stroke of good fortune, he had managed to add the kingship of Macedonia to his realm when Ptolemy arrived at his court. Ptolemy, however, assassinated his protector, and through further murders and internecine strife established himself on the throne. From his violent and unpredictable nature, he bore the nickname 'Keraunus', which meant 'thunderbolt'. Now, with a large Celtic army advancing on his territory, he failed to appreciate the gravity of the situation and—according to Greek writers —behaved like a boastful lunatic.

Celtic emissaries were sent to Ptolemy's court, offering peace if he wished to purchase it. Taking this as a sign that the Celts wished to avoid fighting, Ptolemy boasted that they were afraid of him and demanded that they gift up their arms to him and surrender their chieftains as

Above: The expansion of the Celtic peoples in all directions from the 5th to the 3rd Centuries BC.

Tip of iron lance, with engraving, from an area occupied by early Celtic adventurers moving eastwards along the Danube in the 4th Century BC. Length 11.81in (30cm). Now in Hungarian National Museum, Budapest.

hostages. On hearing news of this, the Celtic leaders broke out into laughter, remarking that 'he would soon see whether they had offered peace for his sake or for theirs'. One report is that Ptolemy actually slew the envoys, thus enraging the Celtic forces further, and then rashly marched out to give battle. The Celts won a resounding victory and decimated the Macedonian army. Ptolemy himself was thrown from his elephant, and the Celtic warriors tore his body to pieces and fixed his head on a lance. It is likely that the Celtic leader got his own nickname from this actual event, for *Bolgios* was the Celtic equivalent of the Greek *Keraunus* for a thunderbolt. After this dramatic success in 279 BC, the Celtic army could well claim that their leader was the real thunderbolt, a designation which moreover was often used for their own god of war.

Panic gripped all of Macedonia, and the gates of the cities were shut, but a minor chief called Sosthenes gathered together the remnants of the Macedonian army and started on a guerrilla campaign against the forces of Bolgios. This caused the Celts to cease their advance and, satisfied with the booty which they had gained, they returned to their base to plan further raids. Meanwhile, the army of Cerethrios was penetrating further south and east, and pushing as far as the Maritsa river in present-day Bulgaria and proceeding from there across the Rodopi Mountains to Thessaly.

Brennos had reached the borders of Greece and, when he heard that Bolgios had not pursued the campaign through Macedonia, he decided to direct his own army there. As he was laying waste the whole Macedonian countryside, Brennos encountered the forces led by Sosthenes and defeated them. The Celts now began to plunder, not only human settlements, but religious temples as well; and Brennos is reputed to have jested that 'the gods being rich ought to be generous to men'.

Sensing total victory, Brennos called public assemblies of the Celts and planned an expedition into Greece. He pointed out to the various Celtic chieftains that Greece, though a very wealthy country, was in a weak military position, and he tempted their greed by reminding them of the immense treasures of gold and silver to be had

ABOVE: Head of Celtic deity, with torc collar, dating from 2nd or 1st Century BC. Found in Holg districty, near Mšecké Žehrovice, in Bohemia. It is of argillaceous slate and is 9.84in (25cm) in height. Now at Národni Muzeum, Prague

there. In this way, in the year 278 BC, Brennos put together a huge army, reportedly of over 150,000 foot and over 20,000 horse, and—accompanied again by his lieutenant Acichorios — headed south for Delphi. In citing these numbers, a later Greek writer states that the actual cavalry strength was over 62,000, and explains this by the fighting tactic which the Celts called trimarcisia ('feat of three horsemen'):

> *The servants remained in the rear, close at hand; if a trooper had his horse killed, the servant brought him a fresh mount; if the trooper himself were slain, the man mounted his master's horse; and if this man too fell, the third servant in turn took his place in the fight. If the master were wounded, one of the servants conveyed him to the camp while the other took his place in the ranks.*

The rapid successes of the Celts had, however, been gained at a diplomatic price, and this became particularly evident in the Greek campaign. The Greeks had observed that the payment of tribute had not protected the Macedonians, Thracians, Paeonians, and Thessalians from devastation. Reasoning that it would not protect them either, the Greeks determined to oppose the invaders to the death. The Celts soon found that in this case they were facing a much more formidable foe than heretofore, and one comparable to Rome which their kinsmen were facing in the great pensinsula to the west of them.

When the army of Brennos entered Greece, they met with no opposition for a while, and advanced towards the pass of Thermopylae, through which entry could be gained from Thessaly into the centre of Greece. The Greeks were determined to defend this narrow pass, not only because of its strategic, but also because of its cultural, importance to them. For it was there that, two centuries before, 300 brave Spartans had, with allies, held at bay an immense army under King Xerxes of Persia, reputed to have numbered several millions.

ABOVE: Greek paestum from the 3rd Century BC, representing a charioteer with racing horses. The Greeks, who had a highly developed equestrian culture, admired the horsemanship of the Celts.

Now, again, Greece was threatened by an army of invasion at Thermopylae, and contingents from several of the Greek states rallied to the defence. The full Greek force was probably about 40,000 strong, and was under the command of the Athenian Callippus.

Learning that Brennos's army had reached Magnesia, they sent a force of a thousand picked footsoldiers and a company of horse to the river Spercheios to impede their approach. They accordingly destroyed all the bridges and encamped on the opposite bank. Brennos, however, had foreseen this, and so he sent 10,000 tall men downriver by night. This would appear to have been Brennos's own personal troop, for the Greek writers—while remarking that 'the Celts as a race are far taller than any other people' —claim that his company 'was composed of the tallest and bravest' of the army. These crossed the river at a broad point, some of them swimming, others wading across, and others using their shields as rafts. When the Greek force on the river-bank realised what had happened, they fell back to rejoin their own body.

Brennos lost no time in having new bridges built over the Spercheios, so that his whole army could cross. He ravaged the countryside, but left the city of Heraclea untouched in his haste to reach Thermopylae. On being informed by deserters that the Greek force was very small by comparison with his own, he offered battle at sunrise on the following day. The Greeks advanced to the pass silently and in close order, and the Celts soon discovered that the pass was so narrow, and the ground so slippery and rocky there, that their cavalry was useless to them in the battle. They also found themselves at a disadvantage with regard to armour, for the Greeks were well-clad while the Celts' only defence was provided by the shield. Hieronymus describes the way in which the Celts fought in this battle:

They rushed on their enemy with the rage and fury and blind courage of a wild beast. Hacked with swords and axes, and pierced with darts and javelins, their fury only died with life itself. Indeed, some even plucked out the weapons that struck them and hurled them back at the Greeks, or used them in hand-to-hand fighting.

Meanwhile, the Greek fleet came as close to the shore as possible, at the rear of the Celts, and raked them with all kinds of missiles and arrows. Soon the Celts—caught between the fire from front and rear and confined on the narrow ground—grew tired and frustrated, and their leaders ordered a retreat. Their losses continued as they withdrew, some of them being trampled and others pushed into the mud and water. As in Italy, they had proved to be no match for a well-organised, disciplined, well-equipped, and tactical fighting force. Only 40 of the Greeks were killed in the battle, whereas the Celtic losses ran into thousands. It is reported that the Greeks buried their own dead and despoiled the corpses of the enemy, whereas the Celts made no effort to bury theirs but left them to be devoured by wild beasts and birds. This was attributed to a wish to strike fear into the Greeks by their callous indifference, but the real reason may have been a religious one, for—as we have seen in Chapter 2—the carrion-crow was a representative of the war-goddess to the Celts.

It is obvious that the battle of Thermopylae was by no means a decisive one, and it was regarded by Brennos as no more than a temporary setback. Six days after the battle, a detachment from the Celtic army began to ascend Mount Oeta by a narrow path from the city of Heraclea. Their objective was the ruins of Trachis, where there was a sanctuary of Athena rich in votive offerings. They were intercepted, however, by the garrison from Heraclea, under the leadership of Telesarchus. In the ensuing battle, Telesarchus was slain, but his men managed to repulse the Celts and to save the shrine. This second defeat dampened the spirit of the Celts further, but Brennos —who was a skilled strategist—determined to persist.

He thought of a plan to draw away from the main Greek force the Aetolians, who numbered something in the region of 10,000 fighting men. The plan was to invade and lay waste the whole of Aetolia, and for this purpose Brennos selected 40,000 foot and 800 horse soldiers, and placed them under the command of Orestorios and Combutis. The force crossed back over the river Spercheios, and passed through Thessaly and on to the town of Callium in Aetolia, which they attacked with a terrible ferocity. Reports began to come back to the Greeks of the wholesale murder of the men-folk in Aetolia, of the rape of women, and even of cannibalism by the Celts. The Aetolian army quickly set out for their homeland, where they were joined by the frantic inhabitants of the towns which had not yet fallen. A force of Patreans from Achaea also came to support them.

As the Celts under Orestorios and Combutis were returning from their destruction of Callium, they were waylaid by this combined Aetolian and Patrean army. The Patreans made a frontal assault on them, and managed to withstand the fierce counter-attack by the Celts. Meanwhile, the Aetolians lined the whole road and kept up a barrage of missiles against the Celts, who had only their shields for protection. Groups of the Celts tried to pursue their tormentors but, failing to catch up with them, were met with renewed attacks on their return to the road. They were harassed all the way back to Thermopylae, and it is reported that less than half of them reached Brennos's camp safely.

BRENNOS'S NEW PLAN FAILS

Brennos now determined on a new plan, to cross Mount Otea—not by the steep path through Trachis, but by a less precipitous one through the territory of the Aenianes. In order to rid themselves of the Celts, the inhabitants of Heraclea as well as the Aenianes offered to guide him. So Brennos set out on this path with 40,000 of his men, leaving the remainder of his force in camp under the command of Acichorios, with orders to attack the Greeks as soon as Brennos himself had got to their rear. It chanced that on that day a thick mist was on the mountain, so that the Phocians, whom the Greeks had posted on the pass, did not see the Celts until they were almost upon them. The Celts overpowered them and drove them from the pass, clearing the way. The Phocians, however, managed to get word of what was happening to the main Greek force, which was transported by sea away from Thermopylae and out of the trap.

Noticing that the Greek army had escaped him, Brennos did not even wait to rejoin forces with Acichorios, but headed straight for Delphi. The terrified inhabitants of that city fled to their celebrated oracle, which reassured them of their safety in the impending danger. The Greek army began to muster again at Delphi, but not in such numbers as before. In their forefront were the Phocians and some Aetolians, while many more of the latter went to impede the army of Acichorios, which was trying to join up with that of Brennos. Acichorios had left part of his force at Heraclea to guard the spoils there, and the Aetolians hung on the rear of his marching force, capturing his baggage and cutting off the men in charge of it.

Brennos himself, meanwhile, had reached Delphi and was being confronted by the main body of Greeks there. The Greek authors report that Apollo, the god of the oracle, gave the message through his priestess: 'I will defend my own!.' One account has the priestess, writhing on her chair and saying with a raging voice that Apollo and 'white virgins' would protect the site. Brennos laughed at this idea that the gods could appear in human shape, but the Greek historians were keen to expose him as a sacriligeous and helpless mortal who tempted fate. So

Athletic Celtic warrior on horseback, depicted on a Gaulish golden coin of the 1st Century BC (diameter 0.8in/22mm). Now at Cabinet des Médailles, Bibliothéque National, Paris.

The sacred centre of Delphi, site of a great votive treasury, and which was reputed to have been protected by the god Apollo from the huge Celtic army of the second Brennos. Celtic traditions claimed that some of the treasure was in fact taken away by them.

we read that, when the battle began, the god Apollo immediately showed signs of his hostility to Brennos. The ground under the Celtic army began to tremble violently, and then thunder and lightning broke out over their heads. Flashes from heaven struck into the middle of them, striking individuals down and setting fire to the shields and clothes of others. To add to their terror, phantoms of great Greek heroes of the past appeared before them, and as night fell it snowed hard. The Greeks interpreted the snowflakes driven into the faces of the Celts as the 'white virgins', and to add to the effect of the blizzard great boulders began to slip down from Mount Parnassus on top of them. Much of this is no doubt poetic elaboration, and the disturbances of earth and sky would seem to be an echo from the Celts' own proverb—discussed in Chapter 1 —that they feared nothing, unless the sky fell upon them and the earth open underneath them.

The position was in reality serious. At break of day the Greeks advanced from Delphi directly towards the enemy. As the surprised Celts came to terms with this, they were attacked from the rear by the Phocians, who descended the steep slopes of Parnassus through the snow. Caught in the crossfire, the Celts nevertheless fought bravely, and particularly the bodyguard of Brennos, whom the Greeks described as 'the finest and bravest men of them all'. Brennos was wounded and carried helpless off the field, and the loss of their leader in this way so disheartened the Celts that they determined on a general retreat. They continued their retreat until nightfall, when they encamped as best they could. The Greek authors claim that they were struck by the fears inspired by Pan—in the evening some of them imagined the sounds of

a hostile army approaching and the hoofbeats of horses charging at them, and this panic spread gradually throughout the whole army. In the darkness they began to mistake each other for Greeks, and in this way fighting broke out among themselves. Observing this from a distance, the Phocians began to renew their pressure on the Celts, and we read that in addition to the loss of 6,000 men in the battle the day before, the Celts lost a further 10,000 in their frantic retreat.

The Phocians saw to it that no supplies were available in the path of the retreating army, so that hunger also set in, causing the deaths of thousands more. Now the Athenians and Boeotians joined in the pursuit, hanging on the flanks of the Celtic army, ambushing sections of them, and cutting off stragglers. Acichorios managed to join forces with Brennos at Heraclea, but by now the strength of the whole Celtic army had been so reduced as to be a mere shadow of its former self. Although his wounds were not of a fatal character, Brennos felt shamed and disgraced at his failure. He called his army together, and advised them to kill himself and all the other wounded, to burn their wagons, and to return home unburdened. He also advised them to make Acichorios their leader, and then committed suicide—probably with a sword, but one source claims by drinking undiluted wine. Acichorius had him buried, and then slew 20,000 of their incapacitated dependents, before setting out for home by the same route that they had come.

The Greeks were elated at the turn of events, and much relieved, and the victory was celebrated at Delphi every four years afterwards with a festival of salvation called the Soteria. Brennos too was long remembered, with a mixture of repulsion and admiration. Because of his looting of temples, he became the archetypal committer of sacrilege, yet he was regarded as a handsome and brave man whose tragic mistake was to interfere with the god Apollo, a deity which it was believed had dealt him three wounds in the battle.

Fleeing Celtic warriors depicted on a terracotta frieze from the temple at Civita Alba, near Sassoferrato in eastern Italy. Now in Museo Civico, Bologna.

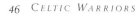

Apollo and the supernatural forces which were reputed to have aligned themselves against Brennos at Delphi were in effect the guardian spirits of the treasures which he attempted to seize there. That his followers did indeed take away much treasure is clear from recorded Celtic tradition. According to this, some of the Tectosages, having returned to their homeland from Delphi, settled at Toulouse in the south of France. A pestilence came upon them there, and they could only recover by following the advice of their wise men to throw the gold and the silver into the lake of Toulouse. In other words, they made a ritual deposit according to their own religious customs of the riches which had earlier been deposited by the Greeks at Delphi.

Little is known of Brennos himself, except that he was of the Tolistobogii tribe, but he obviously was a charismatic leader, and he may have been named after the other great Celtic war-leader of a century before in Italy.

Eventually, the retreating Celts reached the river Spercheios, and after crossing this they were further attacked by the Thessalians and Malians, who wished to avenge former wrongs. Their tormented journey continued northwards, until they reached relatively safer surroundings among their own people who had settled in Thrace. A sequel to this failed campaign was provided by events which occurred in the following year, 277 BC, and again the Celts were the losers. When he had embarked on the invasion of Greece, Brennos had left a force of 15,000 foot and 3,000 horse soldiers to guard the Celts' own frontier. Left leaderless, these now embarked on military adventures of their own, winning battles against the Getae and Triballi, both Thracian peoples.

They then decided to plunder Macedonia once more, but an able soldier, Antigonus Gonatas, was returning from the east to take over the kingship of his country. The Celts sent emissaries to this Antigonus, with the usual offer of peace in return for money, but with the hidden intent of spying on both his wealth and his military strength. The wily Antigonus invited the emissaries to a banquet, and made much show of his wealth and pretended weakness. Inevitably, his camp was soon after raided by the Celts, but he had foreseen all of this and had concealed his army in a neighbouring wood. The army attacked and slaughtered the raiders as they departed with their plunder.

The losses sustained by the Celts in the Greek campaign had been atrocious, but their power in eastern Europe was by no means at an end. The Classical writers bear witness to the fact that they restabilised their power-base in the home territories and held onto their conquests in adjacent territories. Many placenames of that area in ancient times bear witness to the presence of Celtic strongholds, which must have presided over mixed populations of Celtic and earlier inhabitants. The Boii, for instance, founded the the hill-fort settlement of Vindobona (the origin of Vienna), and the Scordisci —a group comprised of various Celtic tribes who took their new name from Mount Scordus—founded an important fortress which they called Singidunum (the origin of Belgrade).

The Scordisci began to expand even further to the east, and one Comontorios, who had been an officer in the army of Brennos, conquered Thrace and established a Celtic kingdom there. They made Tylis their capital, and from there carried out raids for tribute against the Byzantines, as a result of which they gained the reputation of preferring to

The Dying Gaul, a Roman marble copy of a bronze statue erected by King Attalus I of Pergamum, to celebrate his victory over the Galati. The naked warrior is dying from a wound in his right side, and his sword and war-trumpet are also represented. Now in Museo Capitolino, Rome.

steal gold rather than to mine it. The first such attacks were carried out by Comontorius, and his forces were bought off at an enormous cost of thousands of gold pieces. Eventually the Byzantines agreed to pay a yearly tribute of 80 talents in return for security. This continued down until the reign of Cavaros as Celtic king of Thrace.

Polybius says that, in order to raise the money to pay this, the Byzantines put a tax on ships sailing into the Pontus and this was the cause of a war between them and the Rhodians in 220 BC. Cavaros, however, intervened and negotiated a treaty to end the war. This Cavaros (whose name was probably a title meaning 'the huge warrior') was described by Polybius as being 'of a truly royal and high-minded disposition'. The same writer adds, however, that Cavaros was corrupted by a flatterer from Chalcedon called Sostratus, and it was apparently advice from that source which led Cavaros into increasing taxes on the native Thracians, which led to a revolt in 212 BC. In the ensuing fighting, Cavaros was killed and the Celtic kingdom of Thrace was destroyed.

Just as the Celts in Italy were generally known as Galli (literally 'foreigners'), those in eastern Europe were called by a name of similar derivation, Galati. One Classical writer states that the Galati were at that time so numerous that they soon began to swarm into Asia. This is of course an exaggeration, but it is clear that, with their defeat in the southern Balkans, their eyes were turned inevitably towards the east. We read that in the year 278 BC most of the Galati crossed to Asia Minor in ships and plundered its sea-coast. The Roman historian Livy claims that the Celts who went to Asia Minor had departed from the army of Brennos in

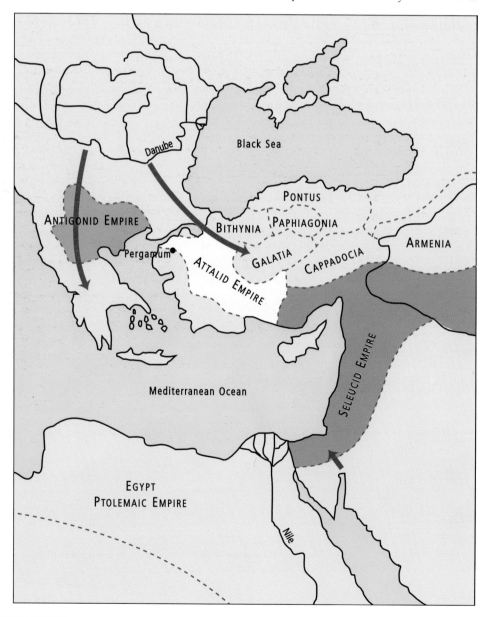

The thrust of the Galati into Asia Minor, and the area of their settlement there in the midst of longer established powers.

Greece due to a disagreement with him. He states that about 20,000 men, under the leadership of Lonorios and Lutarios, left Brennos and went through Thrace to Byzantium. This report seems to be a confusion arising from the complicated series of expansions undertaken by the Celts between the years 281 and 278 BC. It may be that, when Brennos tried to bring together the majority of the Celtic fighters for his invasion of Greece, some who had been involved in Cerethrios's campaign to Thessaly had opted instead to pursue their fortunes in an eastern direction. These would later have been joined in Thrace by remnants of Brennos's army, and the combined force would have undertaken the crossing to Asia.

At any rate, Livy tells us that, having gained control of the coast of Propontis and having imposed tribute on the towns of that area, these Galati were tempted by reports of the riches of Asia. Seizing more territory, they went down to the Hellespont, from where they sent messengers to Antipater, king of Cilicia, who controlled the coast. While waiting for a reply, dissension arose between the two leaders, and Lonorios returned to Byzantium with the largest part of their forces. Lutarios seized some ships from Antipater's delegates and ferried his men in batches across the Hellespont into Asia Minor. Shortly afterwards, Lonorios crossed from Byzantium, having obtained the assistance of the King of Bithynia, Nicomedes.

The two forces then rejoined, and acted as clients in Nicomedes's war against his rival Ziboietes. Nicomedes was successful, largely due to the help of the Celts, but these were dangerous hirelings and proved difficult to satisfy. Disregarding Nicomedes, they advanced further into Asia Minor, receiving tribute from all whom they encountered. The peoples of regions such as Pontus, Paphlagonia, Cappadocia, and Pergamum were weakened by continuous wars, and were in no position to oppose an army of 20,000 men who, even though badly armed, had such a warlike reputation. They threatened major cities like Troy, Ephesus, and Celaenae. Greek legend had it that the people of Themisonion were directed to caverns for safety from the Celts by the gods Herakles, Hermes, and Apollo, and that three virgins of Miletos had committed suicide to avoid being molested by the fearsome raiders.

Celt and wife committing suicide. Marble copy of a bronze statue erected by King Attalus I in a sanctuary at Pergamum in thanks for his victory over the Galati.

There were three major tribes of these 'Galati', and they divided the territory between them - the Tolistoboii in the modern Eskisehir area, the Tectosages east of them in the Ankara area, and the Trocmi east again in the mountainous Kirikalle area. The Tectosages captured the city of Ancyra (modern Ankara), probably with the assistance of Mithridates I, King of Pontus. Antiochus I, the king of Syria, resented the presence of the demanding newcomers, and in 275 BC he crushed them in battle with his elephant-army, as a result of which he gained the Greek title Soter (meaning 'saviour'). The Galati recovered, however, and ten years later gained their revenge by defeating and slaying Antiochus in a battle near Ephesus. Syria no longer threatened the Galati, who actually intervened in a dynastic dispute in 246 BC between the

Syrian king Seleucus II and his brother Antiochus Hierax. The latter engaged the Galati as mercenaries to do most of his fighting and, in an attempt to counter this, Seleucus confronted them in a major battle at Ancyra. The Galati defeated him, and as a result felt free to extend their demands for tribute over an even wider area. Particularly odious was the ransom which was demanded for people who were kidnapped—this was aptly known as Galatika ('Celt-money').

The patience of the rulers of Asia Minor finally began to run out. Among the kingdoms which paid the tribute was Pergamum, but a new leader, Attalus I, succeeded to the throne there in 241 BC. Attalus was determined not to kowtow to plunderers and, when the Galati came to collect their tribute from him in 240 BC, he met them with his army near the source of the river Caice and inflicted a stunning defeat on them. Eight years later, the Tolistoboii thought to avenge this by a raid on Pergamum, but they were met and routed by Attalus close to the city. As a result of these defeats, the Galati were unable to spread their power further east and were, in effect, confined to the area which came to be known from their name as Galatia, in north-central Turkey.

Noting the competence of the Galati as fighters, rulers in the area invited other Celts in as mercenaries, but not always with benign results. For example, the son and successor of the Syrian king Seleucus II, who had been defeated in   battle by the Celts, was not free from the pernicious influence of these outsiders. This king, Seleucus III, planned to counter the growing power of Attalus but, as he advanced with a large army in 223 BC, he was assassinated by one of his own mercenaries, a Celt named Apotouros. His brother and successor again, Antiochus III, was not deterred by this, and kept a large contingent of Celtic mercenaries in his army. In his war against Molon ,satrap of Media, in the year 220 BC, for instance, he had a troop belonging to the Celtic tribe Rhigosages, who were probably imported by him from Europe. When, three years later, he suffered a disastrous defeat at the hands of an Egyptian army led by Ptolemy IV at Rafah on the border of Palestine, that Egyptian army itself had a substantial number of Celtic mercenaries from Thrace in its ranks.

Two years later, Attalus himself hired a large force of mercenaries from the Aegosages, a Celtic tribe from Thrace, and used them in his wars against the Aeolians, Lydians, and Phrygians. He was disappointed with their performance, however, for they disliked the hardship of the long marches and 'despised all authority', and moreover brought their wives and children in wagons with them wherever they went. When an eclipse of the moon occurred, these Celts claimed that it was a bad omen and refused to go on. Attalus therefore had little choice but to allow them to return to where they had crossed into Asia, and he settled them around the

Chalcolithic stele of Celtic warrior, France.

Hellespont. Soon after, however, these Aegosages rebelled and besieged the city of Troy. The siege was raised, and the Aegosages withdrew to Bithynia, where they continued to plunder until defeated by the army of the king of that region, Prusias I, at Arisba. Prusias massacred all of their warriors on the battlefield, and then slew nearly all their women and children in their camp. In describing this action of Prusias, the historian Polybius remarks that it was 'a signal warning for future generations against barbarians from Europe being too ready to cross into Asia'.

The Greek writer Strabo states that the Trocmi and Tolistoboii got their names from their chieftains, whom we may presume were Trocos and Tolistos., respectively. The Tectosages—as we have seen—were a section of the Volcae, one of the most influential tribes of the Celts, and another branch of them was settled in the south of France. Regarding the governmental structure of these Celts who had settled in Galatia, Strabo states that each of the three tribes were divided into four 'tetrarchies'. Their full council, including these 12 leaders, amounted to 300 persons, and they all assembled periodically at a place called 'Drynemeton'. This is probably a corruption of dru-nemeton ('druidic sacred place'), a placename with many parallels throughout the Celtic world, and the custom of assembling at one central shrine to decide on public affairs was known also in Celtic Gaul and in early Ireland.

These Celts of Asia Minor had thus, within a few generations, settled down to a reasonably stable existence, and had brought their culture with them and adapted it to the new environment. They mingled with the native Phrygian people of that area, and all indications are that the Celtic elements predominated in that mix. That is not to say, however, that they devoted themselves totally to agricultural rather than military pursuits. Although their own territorial ambitions had been thwarted, they—in common with the Celts in other areas— soon gained a fearsome reputation as hired soldiers in wars between other peoples.

Chapter 4

SOLDIERS OF FORTUNE

The Greek writer Xenophon describes how Dionysius of Sicily, in assisting his allies in the Peloponnesian War of 369-368 BC, employed Celts and Iberians as mercenaries. About 2,000 of these, along with about 50 horsemen, were sent to assist the Spartans against the Thebans, and they proved very effective. From the account given of their fighting tactics, this small contingent of mounted warriors would appear to have been of the same stock as the infantry. The practice was to scatter them among the rest of the army, from which positions they would make sudden charges on horseback against the Thebans, throw their javelins, and then dash away, turning around abruptly to throw more javelins. They would dismount and rest regularly, and when threatened would leap onto their horses and retreat. They would lead pursuers too far from their own lines, and then wreak havoc on them by a shower of javelins. In this way they could control the entire movements of the opposing army during a battle, and proved to be of great strategic importance. Plato, however, was not as complimentary as Xenophon, and complained that the Celts and Iberians were given to drunkenness, an attribute which he probably noticed while he was at the court of the same Dionysius.

It is probable that some of Dionysus's mercenaries were recruited from Cisalpine Gaul, but most of them seem to have been from Iberia. These would have been representative of the generally mixed population of eastern and central Spain at the time, for Celtic groups had settled there among earlier local peoples, forming what we know as the Celtiberian culture. There are indications that these people were well accustomed to the mercenary way of life, and that—as well as gradually encroaching upon lands to the west and south of the peninsula—many of them also served as hired fighters for the native peoples of these areas, such as Iberes, Lusitani, Carpetani, Vettones, and Vascones

In the 2nd Century BC, the writer Posidonius gave a colourful account of the Celtiberians. He stated that the fusion between Celts and Iberi took place only after long and bloody wars. They were, he said, well known for being very warlike, but also for being very hospitable. 'The Celtiberians wear black clothes, hairy like goatskin. Some have shields of the lightly coloured Celtic type, others have a round shield of the kind more familiar in the Greek world. The iron of their two-edged swords, shorter than the Celtic great sword, is capable of cutting anything.' Posidonius said that they were accustomed to bury a piece of iron in the ground until the softer layers of the metal were rusted away, and they then forged the harder part of the metal into a sword.

Strabo also gives a colourful account of the Celtiberians. He describes them as impulsive and brave, but lazy and indifferent to hygiene—sleeping on the ground and using stale urine to wash themselves and to clean their teeth. Like the Celts of other areas, they mixed infantry and cavalry in their war-troops. 'They have some cavalry interspersed among the foot-soldiers, and the horses are trained to traverse the mountains and to sink down on their knees at the word of command, in case of necessity.' Often, he says, two men mounted on one horse, so that in a conflict one of them could descend and fight on foot.

The major power with which the Celtiberians came into conflict was Carthage. This was a strong north African city, which from the 6th Century BC had been extending its power throughout all the surrounding region, and then began to establish colonies on the other side

of the Mediterranean in the islands of Corsica, Sardinia, and Sicily. The Carthaginians, a Phoenician people, also seized towns on the southern Iberian coast, and set up strongholds there. They engaged mercenaries from different parts of the Mediterranean, including Spartans, Ligurians, and Celtiberians, and, in order to bolster their struggles against the Greeks, made several treaties with Rome. The situation whereby the Carthaginians depended so heavily on mercenaries, however, proved to be risky and unstable.

After Rome had stabilised the situation in northern Italy by repelling the Celtic raids, and then forming settlements in the southernmost territories of Cisalpine Gaul, she turned her attentions to the south of Italy , where the Greeks had for long been ensconced and which for them was known as Magna Graeca. When the city of Tarentum was threatened by the Romans, the Greeks of that area called on a famous general called Pyrrhus to come to their assistance. This Pyrrhus had been king of Macedonia and was now king of Epirus. In the year 280 BC he landed on the south-eastern coast of Italy with an army of 25,000 men and 20 elephants, and soon after routed a much larger Roman army near Heraclea. Marching north to Apulia, he persuaded the Celts of that area to join him, and at Asculum (now Ascoli) he clashed with another large Roman army and defeated it also. However, his own losses in this battle were, so high that he commented afterwards, 'another such victory and we are lost!'

Abandoning his campaign in Italy, he left for Sicily to support the Greek cities there against the Carthaginians, but returned again four years later and raised a new army in Italy comprising Samnites, Greeks, Celts, and others. After his defeat by the Romans at Beneventum, he finally returned to Macedonia, in an attempt to regain his kingdom there from the incumbent Antigonus Gonatus.

This Antigonus, having defeated the Celtic invaders of his country, had enlisted many of them as mercenaries, and these were led by their chieftain Ceredrios. Antigonus even lent a contingent of 4,000 Celtic mercenaries to King Ptolemy II of Egypt, who was at war with his half-brother Magas in 277-276 BC. Ptolemy won his war, but the Celtic corps mutinied against him and attempted to seize his treasures. He besieged them on an uncultivated island in the river Nile, where some of them starved and the rest appear to have committed ritual suicide. Ptolemy was so overjoyed at this success that he had a Gallic shield printed on his coins, and had a great monument constructed which depicted decapitated Celtic warriors. Undeterred by his experience of these hired fighters, he and his successors had more Celts in their employ in later years.

On his return to Macedonia, Pyrrhus was joined by a number of Celtic mercenaries and later by some Macedonians. In 274 BC, he made a surprise attack on the army of Antigonus at the entrance to a narrow defile, causing so much confusion that the elephants of Antigonus were hemmed in and their drivers surrendered. The strong contingent of Celts in Antigonus's army fought bravely, but most of them were slaughtered in the fierce fighting, and soon after the rest of the army surrendered to Pyrrhus. After the battle, Pyrrhus remarked that of all his successes this victory over the Celts was 'the one which added most to his fame'. In commemoration of the victory, he had the long shields of the Celts dedicated to the goddess Athena at a Macedonian sanctuary, while the round shields of the Macedonians themselves were dedicated to Zeus.

Pyrrhus then captured the city of Aegae and garrisoned it with his Celtic troops. The historian Plutarch described what happened then: 'As a race the Celts have an insatiable appetite for money, and they now dug up the tombs of the rulers of Macedonia who are buried there, plundering the treasure and scattering the bones without respect.' Plutarch adds that Pyrrhus refrained from punishing the mercenaries for doing this because he was afraid of them. He lost support through this and other indiscretions and, still supported by his Celtic mercenaries, he was killed in an attack on Sparta in 272 BC —after which Antigonus regained the Macedonian throne, again employing Celtic warriors as mercenaries in his army. In the year 265 BC, however, the Celts who had been stationed by Antigonus in the city of Megara, in the east of Corinth, mutinied because of poor pay. The mutiny was suppressed, and all of the rebels were put to death.

CELTIBERIAN MERCENARIES IN SICILY

Meanwhile, in Sicily, events were taking shape which would involve the Celts in a much bigger way in the struggles of others. There the Romans began to challenge the control by the Carthaginians of most of the island, and they manoeuvred a war against the latter which began in 264 BC and lasted for 13 years. The Romans gained several initial victories but, after an invasion of north Africa, they were disastrously defeated by the Carthaginian army which was led by a Spartan mercenary called Xanthippus. Confining their efforts to Sicily itself thereafter, the Romans won several victories on land and sea and eventually forced the Carthaginians to vacate the island. Thus ended the First Punic War in 241 BC.

Most of the fighters in the Carthaginian army in Sicily had been Celtiberian mercenaries, and their reputation was not good. Polybius states that they had committed treachery against their own people and had been expelled from Iberia, but the Carthaginians had taken them on board and posted them as a garrison in Agrigentum (now Girgenti). A dispute over pay gave them the opportunity to plunder that city, following which they were posted to the Carthaginian force under the command of Hamilcar Barca on the steep slopes of Mount Eryx (now Giuliano). The Carthaginians were besieging the Roman fortress on the summit, but were in turn being besieged by a Roman force at the foot of the mountain. Disliking this assignment, about 800 of the Celtiberian mercenaries lost no time in deserting to the Romans. As soon as the war was over, the Romans put these on board ship and forbade them to land in Italy. The renegades were eventually accepted at Epirus in Greece, but within a few years they deserted their new employers and betrayed that city to the Illyrians.

After the peace was concluded in Sicily, the Carthaginian leaders Hamilcar Barca and Gisgo arranged to transport the remainder of their mercenaries from that island back to Africa. Gisgo planned to bring them over in groups, so that each group could be paid off and sent to their own country before they could cause trouble at Carthage. In an attempt to save money, however, the government at Carthage did not dismiss the various detachments as they landed but detained all the mercenaries together in the hope that they would accept less than their full pay. This was an ill-judged policy, for the mercenaries grew restless and began to commit

RIGHT: The boy Hannibal swearing eternal hostility to Rome. His father Hamilcar Barca agreed to allow him to travel with the new Carthaginian army to Spain on condition that he swore such an oath. From a fanciful painting by Benjamin West.

depredations in the city. They were ordered to withdraw in one great mass to the town of Sicca. When a further attempt was made to decrease the payment due to them, the mercenaries revolted. They consisted principally of Celtiberians, Ligurians, Balearics, and Greeks. Buoyed by their exploits against the Roman legions in Sicily, they advanced on Carthage, and Polybius states that 'not only was it impossible for the Carthaginians to face them in battle, but it would be difficult to find any nation in the world who could'. The Carthaginians made many more promises, but by this stage the mercenaries could not be placated.

Their leaders were a runaway Roman slave called Spendius with a force of mixed nationalities totalling 6,000 men, a Libyan soldier called Matho, and a Celt called Autaritos

with 2,000 of his nationality. Their plan was to conduct their campaign from the slopes of the mountains, where the Carthaginians could not use their elephants and heavy armaments. Thus began 'the truceless war', which lasted for 40 months, with atrocious acts of cruelty on both sides. The rebels, whose tactics were successful for a long time, seized many towns and were joined by a huge force of Libyans, who wished to assert their country's independence from the oppression of Carthage. The Carthaginian forces were led initially by Hanno, but after repeated failures on his part he was replaced by Hamilcar Barca, whose desperation was so great that he abandoned Sardinia to the Romans in return for their neutrality.

A superb tactician, Hamilcar managed to lure the rebel army onto the plains and defeated them in several battles. In these dire straits, Polybius describes a speech given by the Celtic leader Autaritos, an experienced soldier who had learned the Phoenician language and therefore could communicate very effectively with all the rebel army. He spoke strongly against any compromise, and recommended that all the Carthaginian prisoners be slain.

ABOVE: Hamilcar Barca executing the mercenaries who had rebelled against their Carthaginian employers at the end of the 1st Punic War. Celtiberian fighters were to the fore in this rebellion, which was ruthlessly crushed. From a fanciful painting by G Surand.

Eventually Hamilcar contrived to trap the rebel army near the city of Carthage itself and, with supplies cut off, the rebels were reduced to cannibalism in order to survive. Spendius, Autaritos and some other leaders went to discuss a surrender with Hamilcar, but they were treacherously seized on his orders and crucified on the city walls in full view of their own army. The rebellion collapsed soon after.

A dying Gaulish warrior, from the terracotta frieze in the temple at Civita Alba, near Sassoferrato in eastern Italy. Now at Museo Civico, Bologna.

Hamilcar Barca now turned his attention to the Iberian peninsula, where the emboldened Celts had begun to threaten the Carthaginian colonies. He crossed over in 237 BC, at the head of a formidable army, accompanied by his nine-year-old son Hannibal. As he advanced northwards along the eastern coast, Hamilcar clashed with local Celtiberian fighters, but his army was too large for them to cause any serious problem. By a combination of war and diplomacy, he extended the power of the Carthaginians from Cadiz over all the southern half of the Peninsula until he was slain in battle by the Vettones in the year 229 BC. He was succeeded by his son-in-law Hasdrubal, who founded the city of Cartagena at the south-eastern corner of Spain, a port of great strategic importance as it faced Carthage itself across the sea.

The Romans now began to notice that the Carthaginians had been using Spain to rebuild their power, but felt unable to counter-act this for the moment due to a new threat which was being posed in Italy itself. This was from the Celts of Cisalpine Gaul, from whom a fresh campaign against Rome was imminent. The wily Romans therefore made a treaty with Hasdrubal, according to which the Carthaginian army undertook not to cross the river Ebro. This, in effect, left almost the whole of the Iberian peninsula in the sphere of influence of Carthage.

After their terrible struggles against the Romans, the Celts had been comparatively quiet in their areas of northern Italy for 45 years, but a new generation was now growing up which—according to Polybius — was 'absolutely without experience of suffering or peril'. Some young chieftains made contact with their relatives on the other side of the Alps, inviting them to come and join them in a new war against the Romans. Such a force of Transalpine Celts advanced south as far as Ariminum (now Rimini) in the year 236 BC, and threatened the Roman colony there, but the local Celtic population resented their presence. The Boii killed their own leaders Atis and Galatos, who were in sympathy with the newcomers, and as a result fighting broke out between these two groups of Celts, with great mutual slaughter. The Romans, who had dispatched a legion to the area, looked on in relief as the danger to themselves thus receded. Five years later, the Romans carved up the territory of the Senones among their own settlers, and the Celts began to fear that Rome no longer made war on them for the sake of supremacy, but with a view to their total destruction. The Boii were the most concerned, for their territories were next in line.

In the year 231 BC, the two largest Celtic tribes, the Insubres and Boii, made a compact and sent invitations to a dramatic new group of Celts who were converging in the western Alps and near the river Rhône. These were the Gaesatae ('javelin-men'), an emerging band of professional fighters drawn from different tribes. This new group was probably based on a young warriors' cult which developed into a large force prepared for fighting expeditions. The leaders of the Gaesatae were Concolitanus and Aneroestus. The Insubres and the Boii pointed out to these leaders what great treasures could be had at Rome, and encouraged them by referring to how their own ancestors had once seized that great city. They found ready listeners, and Polybius states that as a result 'on no occasion has that district of Gaul sent out so large a force or one composed of men so distinguished in battle'.

Aware of what was happening, the alarmed Romans were making frantic preparations for the coming storm, even before the Gaesatae had yet left their home bases. Finally, in the year 225 BC, the Gaesatae gathered their forces and crossed the Alps into Italy, where they joined up with their Insubres and Boii hosts. The Romans, however, had persuaded the Veneti in the north-east and the Celtic Cenomani into an alliance with themselves, so that the advancing Celtic army had to leave part of their forces behind them to protect their territories from these. The Romans called up all their available forces, and called to their support also other peoples of central Italy who were alarmed at the apprach of so large a foreign army. The Celtic force numbered in all 50,000 foot and 20,000 cavalry and chariots, and it headed towards Ariminum (now Rimini). There, four Roman legions awaited them, numbering over 20,000 in all, with well over 100,000 allies and support troops, and with hundreds of thousands more spread out from there all the way to Rome.

The Celts March On Rome

Nevertheless, the Celts entered Etruria without any opposition, and decided to march directly on Rome itself. Reaching the city of Clusium, they got news that a large Roman force was approaching, so they encamped there. At nightfall, they lit their camp-fires and retired under the cover of darkness, leaving their cavalry to give the impression that they had not moved. The Romans were duped and, when they saw the cavalry departing, they presumed that the whole Celtic army was in flight. The Celts were awaiting them at a town called Faesulae (now Fiesole), where they ambushed the Romans, who lost 6,000 men in the fighting and were forced to seek refuge on a hill-top. The Celts besieged them there, but a huge Roman army under Lucius Aemilius hastened to the relief. Realising what was happening, the Celtic leader Aneroestes recommended a retreat to their own territories, since they were too encumbered by the great amount of booty they had taken and could return presently in greater preparation to face the Romans. Accordingly, the Celtic army broke up their camp at daybreak and retreated north along the sea-coast of Etruria.

The Roman army of Lucius hung on their rear as the Celts retreated. All went well for the Celts until their advance guard encountered another Roman army, under the command of Gaius Atilius, which had crossed from Sardinia and was marching south from Pisa. Gaius encamped his army on a hill near Telamon and, when they observed that they were caught between two Roman armies, the surprised Celts decided to make a stand there. They deployed their infantry to face in both directions, with the Taurisci and Boii opposing that of Atilius in front, and the Gaesatae and the Insubres defending the rear against Aemilius. They stationed their wagons and chariots at the fore of each front, and placed their booty under guard on a neighbouring hillock.

Polybius describes the appearance of their army thus: 'The Insubres and Boii wore their trousers and light cloaks, but the Gaesatae had discarded these garments owing to their proud confidence in themselves and stood naked, with nothing but their weapons, in front of the whole army.' He explains this behaviour of the Gaesatae was caused by the fact that the ground was overgrown with brambles which would catch in their clothes and impede them. There is no doubt but that fighting stark-naked gave more agility to these young warriors, but the real reason for the tactic was that, by their apparent craziness, they could strike extra fear into the foe. Indeed, like other ancient peoples, the Celts had a strong belief that war-fury gave extra strength to men engaged in combat.

The initial fighting was against the army of Gaius for possession of the hill, around which the Celtic and Roman cavalries were fighting a pitched battle. Gaius himself was slain, and his head was brought as a trophy to the Celtic commanders. After a bitter struggle, however, the Roman cavalry prevailed, and the respective infantries now closed on each other. The Celts, between the two Roman armies, were in a dangerously congested situation, but it could be turned to advantage given the ferocity of their fighters. The Romans, according to Polybius, 'were terrified by the fine order of the Celtic host and the dreadful din, for there were innumerable trumpeters and horn-blowers and, as the whole army were shouting their war-cries at the same time, there was such a tumult of noise that it seemed that not only the trumpets and the warriors but all the surrounding countryside had got a voice and had caught up the cry.' This description echoes the purpose of the Celts, who had a belief that the elements themselves could be harnessed to events taking place on the human level.

A bronze trumpet found in a pond at Loch na Séad, Co Armagh, Ireland. It dates from about the 1st Century BC. Such trumpets were used by the Celts for ritual puposes, and also to terrify the foe in battle. (Ardmhusaem na hÉireann, Dublin.)

The appearance and the gestures of the Gaesatae added greatly to the terror felt by the Romans. These naked warriors were 'all in the prime of life, and finely built men, and all in the leading companies, richly adorned with gold torques and armlets'. As the Gaesatae advanced to throw their javelins, however, their bodies—unprotected but for their shields—were easily targetted by the Roman missiles, until in final desperation they rushed madly on the enemy, only to be cut down mercilessly. They were replaced in the onslaught by Insubres, Boii and Taurisci fighters, and despite terrible losses these more conventional warriors kept up a hand-to-hand combat with the Romans for a long time.

Having lost the initiative through the defeat of the Gaesatae, the Celts were at a great disadvantage, for their shields were much smaller than those of the Romans, and their swords were only serviceable for cutting and not for thrusting. When the Roman cavalry launched a fierce attack from the higher ground on their flank, the Celtic cavalry was put to flight, and the infantry was left unprotected from that quarter. Finally the Celtic ranks broke completely, with about 40,000 slain, and at least 10,000 taken prisoner. Among those captured was Concolitanus, while Aneroestus escaped with a few followers, and then committed suicide.

The Celts had lost their last great battle in Italy and, soon after, the Romans undertook the inevitable invasion of the lands of the Boii, pillaging and destroying as they went. The prisoners were paraded through the streets of Rome to celebrate the triumph, and the Celtic standards and golden torques were sent to adorn the Capitol. Now the Romans decided to pursue their military advantage, and they organised a campaign to take control of the whole valley of the Po. The Boii were forced to submit, and then—with the aid of the Celtic Anari and Cenomani—the Romans attacked the territory of the Insubres.

The chieftains of the Insubres determined on a last stand with a force of 50,000 men on the banks of the Po in the year 223 BC. The Romans, cautious at the prospect of fighting against such a large force, and suspicious that their Celtic allies might change sides, sent these allies first across the river into the attack. They then crossed the river themselves, destroying the bridges behind them. Polybius says that the Roman leaders had noted the age-old vulnerability of the Celts in prolonged struggle, and that their swords were easily bent and needed to be reshaped against the ground by the foot in the heat of battle. The Romans thus instructed their men to first use their javelins, and then resort to their swords before the Celts had repaired their own. In the ensuing battle, the Insubres slashed with their swords, 'which is the peculiar and only stroke of the Celts, as their swords have no points'. With their backs to the river, the Romans used their own swords to great effect on the breasts and faces of their opponents, and gained a decisive victory.

In the following year, the Celts of Italy appealed for peace under any conditions, but this was refused by the new Roman consuls Marcus Claudius and Gnaeus Cornelius. In desperation, the Celts again sent requests for new Gaesatae from the banks of the Rhône in Transalpine Gaul, and they managed to hire a large number of these. The Romans besieged a town called Acerrae between the Po and the Alps, and the Insubres—unable to lift the siege—crossed the Po in retaliation and laid

Bronze Illyrian sculpture of a Celtic warrior, naked except for helmet, collar, and belt. He is in the act of throwing a javelin. The statuette dates from the late 3rd Century BC, and probably represents one of the mercenaries called Gaesatae (literally 'javelin-men').

siege to the town of Clastidium (now Schiattezzo) in the territory of the Anari, a Ligurian tribe who were in alliance with the Romans. Marcus Claudius set out with a cavalry force to relieve this siege, and the Insubres advanced to intercept him. The Roman cavalry prevailed, and the Insubres retired to Mediolanum (Milan), their stronghold. Gnaeus brought his army there to besiege them, but the Celts attacked his rear, putting many of his soldiers to flight. The Romans rallied, however, and defeated the main body of the Insubres and took the fortress. The leaders of the Insubres had no choice but to surrender, and soon afterwards almost all the Celts were expelled from the valley of the Po into the foothills of the Alps to the north and into the Appennines to the west. Polybius states that the Celts lost because all their decisions had been governed 'by the heat of passion rather than by cool calculation'.

The Romans, now unchallenged masters of Italy, could at last turn their attention to countering Carthaginian ambitions in Spain. Events suddenly took an unexpected turn there, for in the year 221 BC, Hasdrubal was assassinated in his dwelling at night by a Celtiberian captive whose master he had executed. The assassin was seized immediately and put to death with hideous tortures, but he showed no sign either of fear or remorse. Livy states that 'even under torture the expression on his face never changed, and one could imagine that triumph had so far subdued his pain that he was actually smiling'.

The man appointed to succeed Hasdrubal as chief commander of all the armies of Carthage was Hamilcar's son Hannibal, who was twenty-four years old and had served as commander of the cavalry in Spain for some years. Hannibal immediately undertook the final subjugation of all Spain. He met with complete success in campaigns against the semi-Celtic peoples such as the Olcades, Vaccaei, and Carpetani, and then directed his attentions to the city of Saguntum (now Sagunto), on the eastern coast. This was a Graeco-Latin colony and was in alliance with Rome.

Hannibal, who had been preparing for a conclusive contest with Rome, decided to provoke a quarrel between the Saguntines and the neighbouring tribes, such as the semi-Celtic Turdetani, which would give him a pretext to attack Saguntum. The tactic worked and, much to the alarm of the Romans, he began the attack on Saguntum in 219 BC and took it with great slaughter eight months later. The Roman Senate immediately declared war on Carthage, and so the Second Punic War had begun. In this great struggle between the two giants of the ancient world, the Celts were by no means an insignificant factor, and both sides made strenuous efforts to gain their support.

Envoys were immediately dispatched by the Roman Senate to Spain, in the hope of bringing the various peoples of that area into an alliance with them. They met with little success, however, being ordered off by the Volciani with the assertion that Rome's word could not be trusted. The envoys then approached the Celts of Transalpine Gaul, asking them to resist the Carthaginians if Hannibal were to bring his army through their territory to attack Italy. The envoys were alarmed at the sight of these Celts attending the council in full armour, as was their custom. The Roman request was met with roars of laughter and derision by the young warriors present, and again the envoys were dismissed with reminders of how the Romans were expelling and oppressing 'men of their nation' in Italy. The only support which the envoys got was from the Greek colonists at Marseilles, who informed them that Hannibal had already won most of the Celts over to his side.

In the spring of the year 218 BC Hannibal made his move. Leaving his brother Hasdrubal to hold Spain with troops from north Africa, he crossed the river Ebro with a force of 90,000 foot, 20,000 horse, and 37 elephants. He was careful to send delegates ahead with promises and

Duel at the battle of Clastidium between Viridomarus, an Insubres leader, and the Roman consul Marcus Claudius Marcellus. Marcus Claudius is said by the Roman writers to have personally slain his opponent. From his victory he gained the Spolia opima, *a guerdon that fell to only two other generals in the history of Rome. (From a fanciful painting by J H Vaida.)*

bribes to guarantee safe passage through the various Celtic territories. Reaching the Pyrenees, he left a force of 10,000 men to guard the passes there, for he mistrusted the independent spirit of the Celtic peoples. He encountered his first major problem after crossing the Pyrenees, for the Celts of that area became alarmed by the approach of so large an army, and a number of them assembled in arms at Ruscino (Rousillon) to oppose him. Hannibal above all else wished to avoid a delay, and so he invited their leaders to his camp and won their approval with protestations of friendship and with gifts.

In Italy, the Boii heard of the passage of Hannibal through Transalpine Gaul, and they encouraged their Insubres neighbours to join them once again in a revolt against Rome. They immediately attacked two new Roman settlements which had been made at Placentia (Piacenza) and Cremona, in their territories, and drove the settlers and the Roman officials headlong before them to the city of Mutina (Modena), which they then blockaded. They next invited the Roman officials to negotiations at their camp outside Mutina, and then seized them as hostages. A relief force under Lucius Manlius was twice ambushed in the woods by the Celts, and badly mauled. Over a thousand Romans were slain in these encounters, and the remainder struggled on to Tannetum, near the Po, where they fortified a position with the help of some Celts from Brescia. The Roman Senate, foreseeing a Celtic uprising to coincide with Hannibal's approach, sent Gaius Atilius with a whole legion and 5,000 allies to the area, and the Celts wisely abandoned both sieges and retired further north.

HANNIBAL SURPRISES THE ROMANS AND THEIR VOLCAE ALLIES

Meanwhile, Cornelius Scipio was dispatched from Rome with a large naval force to Marseilles to impede the progress of Hannibal. Scipio sent out a party of 300 cavalry, with local guides and a pro-Roman Celtic contingent, to reconnoitre. They discovered that Hannibal had come as far as the territory of the Volcae (the region around Toulouse), and that most of the Volcae had decided to resist him and with this purpose had withdrawn to the eastern side of the river Rhône. Some of the Volcae and other neighbouring tribes, however, took the opposite view in their eagerness to be rid of Hannibal and his large army as soon as possible. These latter assembled a large number of boats, canoes and rafts to bring the Carthaginians across. Foreseeing what was going to happen on the far side, Hannibal secretly sent one of his senior officers with a force of Celtiberians to cross the river further north and to descend at the rear of the Volcae. As the Carthaginian army crossed the river, the Volcae warriors came to the opposite bank to oppose them 'howling and chanting as their custom was, shaking their shields above their heads and brandishing their spears', but they were surprised to hear the shouts of the other Carthaginians behind them. They stood their ground for a while, but soon had no choice but to force their way out of the trap as best they could and disperse.

Hannibal was pleased at the outcome and, determined not to be hindered by the Roman forces assembled at Marseilles, he turned north and proceeded along the Rhône valley towards central Gaul until he reached the Aygues river at the western foot of the Alps. This neighbourhood, between the Rhône and its two tributaries, the Ouveze and the Drôme, was known as 'the island', and was very productive of corn. It was inhabited by the Allobroges, one of the strongest and most numerous of the Celtic tribes.

It happened, at that time, that two brothers were contending for the kingship of the Allobroges. One of these, Brancos, was already king, and had the support of the tribal council and elders, but the younger brother had the support of the ambitious young nobles. Hannibal was invited to arbitrate on the issue, and he astutely ruled in favour of the stronger of the two, Brancos. In return, Brancos gave provisions and suitable clothing to the Carthaginian army.

Hannibal set out without delay, still heading north and without hindrance through the territories of other Celtic peoples, the Tricastini, Vocontii and Tricorii. He crossed the Drôme with some difficulty, for it had an unstable stony bed and was in flood. Turning left, he soon reached the foothills of the Alps. As he approached the high mountains, he found the precipices held against him by Celtic tribesmen of that area, but his own Celtic guides discovered for him that by night most of these were wont to disperse to their homes. Giving the impression that his army had camped, therefore, he went with a force of light infantry up the mountains under the cover of dark and soon cleared the pass and gained the higher ground. When the full force of tribesmen returned the next day, they found the Carthaginian army ascending through the pass. The tribesmen, who were used to the terrain and therefore very

Hannibal leading his army across the Alps. An imaginative woodcut by Heinrich Leutemann (1824-1905); number 13 in the series Bilder aus dem Alterthume (Braun & Scneider: Munchen)

surefooted, swarmed down upon the huge army, creating a terrible din. The Carthaginian horses in particular were driven wild by the war-cries and the javelins, and several of these plunged over the cliffs, taking many men with them. Seeing this, Hannibal descended from his own higher position and, with one charge, put the tribesmen to flight. The Carthaginians then seized the village of these tribesmen, and took all their cattle and grain.

Moving on through the mountains, Hannibal met with the elders from other villages, who came to him 'with branches and garlands' as signs of friendship, and offering cattle and hostages to him. This was a trick, and Hannibal was not deceived, though he pretended to be. As he had suspected, his army was attacked in a high mountain pass a few days later. Again from above, the tribesmen struck at his front and rear, rolling rocks down from the heights, and then leaping into the fray throwing missiles. In trying to protect his rear, which had not yet entered the pass, Hannibal found himself cut off overnight from the bulk of his army, but next day he managed to make a juncture again between the divided forces. His army got through, but sustained further losses in driving the enemy away. Following that, across the Alps, the raids made by local tribesmen were for purposes of plunder only, harassing the front and rear of the Carthaginian army and attacking stragglers in particular. These Celtic groups hestitated to launch any more large-scale attacks on the huge army, and they were especially frightened by the prospect of Hannibal's elephants, a kind of animal that they had never seen before.

Hannibal Exhorts His Troops To Be As Courageous As Celts

Finally, as the winter snow began to fall, Hannibal and his army got sight of Italy. They descended the Alps with great hardship. The Roman consul, Cornelius Scipio, whom Hannibal had eluded in Marseilles, came to oppose him, having taken over the troops of Manlius and Atilius who were still reeling from their recent battles with the Boii and Insubres. Hannibal, for his part, was quick to seize upon the dissatisfaction of the Cisalpine Gauls, for his arrival in Italy coincided with the outbreak of hositilies between the Taurini people of Liguria and the Insubres. As soon as his Carthaginian army had recovered from the deprivations of their Alpine crossing, Hannibal attacked and took by storm the chief town of the Taurini (modern Turin), and would have secured the Insubres as allies but for the rapid Roman advance.

Many of the Insubres were forced to serve in the Roman army, while the others withdrew to comparative safety. Nevertheless, Hannibal continued his attempts to attract various Celtic tribes of Italy to his side, instructing his foraging parties to refrain from taking property from them in particular. The Carthaginian and Roman armies finally met at the river Ticino, which flows from the Alps into the Po. As he prepared his army for the battle, Hannibal kindled the ferocity of his own troops by a display which showed his true feelings of superiority towards the natives.

Some Celtic prisoners had been captured in the Alpine fighting, and had been subjected to great hardships—having been flogged mercilessly, half-starved, and kept in heavy chains. Hannibal now had these men brought forward in the full view of his whole army, and had prizes exhibited. The prizes included 'some suits of Gaulish armour, such as are worn by their kings when they engage in single combat', as well as some horses and military cloaks. 'He then asked these young prisoners which of them were willing to fight with each other on the condition of the conqueror taking these prizes and the defeated escaping all his present miseries through death'. Lots were arranged to select those who would contend in the combats. The young prisoners behaved in a truly heroic manner, answering loudly that they would all fight, and 'each one prayed the gods that he might be one of those to draw the lots'. When the combats were over, the surviving captives congratulated the ones who had fallen no less than the victors, 'as having been freed from many terrible sufferings, which they themselves remained to endure'. Hannibal then made a homily of this frightful scene, encouraging his soldiers to fight the Romans with the same sense of desperation as the prisoners had fought each other.

In the ensuing battle, the Carthaginian army triumphed, inflcting heavy casualties on that of Scipio, who retreated in haste to the other side of the river. Most of Hannibal's losses in this battle consisted of his Celtic allies, almost a thousand of them. As a result of his victory, however, many more Celts from the vicinity came to him, offering to join his force and bringing provisions. He received them cordially, and proceeded quickly to Placentia, where he besieged the army of Scipio. There another group of Celts took a hand in affairs. This group consisted of over 2,000 who had been conscripted into Scipio's army, and they now slew the sentries at the

Hannibal meets some of the Celtic chiefs after he had crossed the Pyrenees on his way to Rome. Hannibal kept his relationship with many Celtic tribes friendly so that his passage was smoother and his avenue of retreat more secure. (From an imaginative painting by H. Perrault.)

Roman camp and deserted to Hannibal. He welcomed them, and sent them off to their own communities to incite their people against the Romans.

Most of the Celts, however, remained cautious still, earning the indignation of Hannibal, who stated—with more guile than honesty—that it was the Celts themselves who had invited him into Italy to liberate them. Eventually he lost his patience, and ordered that the whole district as far as the Po be pillaged. In desperation, the Celts appealed to the Romans for help, but Scipio was lukewarm in his response, for a weakened Celtic population was suitable to his interests. The other and recently arrived Roman consul, Sempronius, however, considered that this was a good way to secure the loyalty of the Celts, and he engaged the Carthaginian raiders and repulsed them. In his preparations for a clash with Hannibal, Sempronius used spies from among the Celts for - as Livy states - 'it was safer to use Gauls in this capacity, as they were serving in both camps'.

Hannibal and Sempronius clashed on the river Trebia on a snowy day, and during the course of the battle Hannibal turned his elephants against the Cenomani, the only large-scale Celtic group which was in the Roman army. The Cenomani, who were on the left flank, broke and fled, causing consternation among the Romans, who now had no way out but to go straight through the centre of the Carthaginian army. At that centre, with the African troops, were Celtic contingents; the Romans sustained heavy losses in getting through and were lucky not to have lost their entire army.

The Carthaginian army now headed south through Etruria, enduring terrible hardships because of the bad weather and the lack of proper provisions. Those to suffer most were the Celtic allies, whom Hannibal distrusted and regarded as being lazy and impetuous, and who were unused to such long marches in difficult terrain. They became restless, and would have deserted but for the fact that the African cavalry watched them closely from behind. Hannibal himself feared that they were plotting to assassinate him, and took to wearing various disguises as a precaution.

Other successes for the Carthaginians followed, the most dramatic being at Lake Trasimene, where the new consul Flaminius walked straight into a trap set by Hannibal. In the ferocious fighting, a horseman of the Insubres, called Ducarios, recognised Flaminius and charged straight at his personal bodyguard. Shouting that Flaminius was a destroyer of his nation, Ducarios swore to 'offer him as a sacrifce to the ghosts of our people who were foully slain!' He cut down the armour-bearer who tried to stop him, and then drove his lance through the body of Flaminius himself. He would have stripped the corpse, but was prevented from doing so by Roman shields. After the death of their leader, the Roman army turned and fled, 15,000 of them being slain.

Rome was now in a state of terror as Hannibal advanced swiftly through Umbria and scored his famous victory over a huge Roman army at Cannae. In that battle, his left flank consisted of

Gaulish and Celtiberian cavalry, and at the forefront of the centre he had positioned infantry drawn from the same people. The Gauls, who were naked to the waist, had long swords for slashing; while the Celtiberians, clad in white tunics bordered with purple, had shorter swords for stabbing. As soon as hostilities began, the Celtic horsemen on the flank dashed at the Romans, grappled man-to-man at close quarters and, dismounting from their horses, continued to fight on foot. The superior numbers of the Romans began to prevail, however, and then the Celts at the centre took the main brunt of the Roman assault, being slaughtered in their thousands, and serving Hannibal's master-plan to bring the enemy into the centre where he could outflank and surround them. As a result, the Romans were cut to pieces, losing almost 50,000 men. Again most of the losses on the Carthaginian side were Celts, over 4,000 of them.

After this victory, Hannibal had the upper hand in Italy, but he was too cautious and postponed a direct march on Rome itself. He thus allowed the enemy to reorganise, which they did with great precision according to the advice of the celebrated Quintus Fabius. Hannibal had lost the initiative, and the Romans henceforth were able to contend with him on equal terms.

In that same year of confusion, 216 BC, the Boii took their opportunity, for when a Roman army of 25,000 men under Lucius Postumius tried to enter Italy from the Adriatic coast, these Celts lay in wait for them in the forest which they called Litana. They had the trees by the roadside almost cut through at the base and, as soon as the legions of Postumius marched by, they knocked the trees over on top of them. Then the Boii jumped in among the terrified soldiers and slew them with swords. The body of Postumius himself was stripped, and his head was cut off and taken by the Boii to their temple along with the rest of the spoils. They decorated the skull with gold, and used it as a holy vessel. This accords with the Celtic custom of honouring the heads of fallen enemies, a practice described by Diodorus Siculus, quoting Posidonius, as follows:

> They cut off the heads of enemies slain in battle and attach them to the necks of their horses. They hand over these bloody spoils to their servants to carry off as booty, while striking up a paean and singing a song of victory, and they nail them up as first fruits upon their houses. ... They embalm in cedar-oil the heads of the most distinguished enemies, and preserve them carefully in a chest, and display them with pride to strangers — saying that for this head one of their ancestors, or a man's father, or the man himself, refused the offer of a large sum of money. They say that some of them boast that they refused the weight of the head in gold.

The destruction of Postumius's army caused alarm in Rome, with the one great fear of a combined Celtic and Roman assault appearing to materialise. The Celtic resurgence had come too late, however, for Hannibal was beginning to encounter difficulties further south. He held on for several years in the hope that his brother Hasdrubal would bring another army from Spain over the Alps into Italy. Things had not gone so well for the Carthaginians in Spain, where the Romans were gaining more success in enticing the Celtiberians over to their side. Helped by the Greek colony at Marseilles, a Roman army was ferried by sea to Spain in 217 BC, and these advanced as far south as the Ebro. In the same year a large group of Celtiberians went into an alliance with the commander of this Roman army, Gnaeus Scipio, and took three towns from the Carthaginians. They then engaged Hasdrubal himself and, fighting magnificently, slew 1,500 of his men and took 4,000 prisoners.

While Hasdrubal was thus engaged in fighting the Celtiberians, a second Roman fleet landed, under the command of Publius Scipio, brother of Gnaeus. Soon after an event of major diplomatic importance occurred. Before his departure, Hannibal had been given the sons of many Celtiberian leaders as hostages and these were being held in Saguntum, but they were now handed back to their parents by an Iberian named Abilyx, who was trusted by the Carthaginians but who had entered into communion with the Romans. This development brought more of the Celtiberians over onto the Roman side, so that they were now to be found in almost equal numbers in the armies of both super-powers. In 213 BC, the Romans gained an

Iberian soldier with a long shield and the type of sword known as machaera Hispana. *From a relief on stone at Urso in the south of Spain. Now in Museo Arqueológico, Madrid.*

important victory south-west of Saguntum against a Carthaginian force which consisted mostly of Celts. The latter lost almost 8,000 men, and two of their chieftains, called Moenicaptus and Vismarus, were slain. The Romans collected a huge amount of golden collars and bracelets from the fallen Celtic warriors.

The Romans took Saguntum itself, and wreaked vengeance on the Turdetani tribe, who had started the war, by selling most of them into slavery. Though the two Scipios were slain in separate engagements soon after, the Roman successses continued when Publius Scipio's son, named after his father, was given command. Finally, in the year 210 BC, Cartagena itself fell. The Carthaginians still had three large armies in the Iberian Peninsula, however, and with these they managed to keep the Roman forces tied down there. At long last, in the year 207 BC, Hasdrubal succeeded in getting his army north and crossed the Alps without difficulty, but he was defeated and slain in the north of Italy.

More and more of the Celtiberians continued to go over to the Romans, and an episode in the year 206 BC shows how close to Roman interests the Celtiberians had become. It happened that the Roman commander, the younger Publius Scipio, was staging a public festival at Cartagena in honour of his father and uncle, who had been killed six years before. Many Celtiberians volunteered to take part in a gladiatorial show, some of them being sent by their chieftains to show their valour and others simply enjoying the excitement of fighting. Some others also used the occasion to settle old rivalries, and among these were two cousins who were contending for a chieftainship in the town of Ibes. The older of the two, called Corbis, by his skill easily mastered the strength of the younger man, Orsua, and slew him.

An attempt to assert the independence of the Iberian people from both Rome and Carthage was made in the year 205 BC by two leaders, Indibilis and Mandonius. These had some Celtic support, but they were defeated with heavy losses by the Romans. Meanwhile, the great war was coming to a close, as Romans landed a strong force in Africa in 204 BC and began to attack Carthage itself. The Carthaginian forces were in hasty retreat, but they were rallied and greatly heartened by the arrival from Spain of a 4,000 strong force of Celtiberians, who had been newly recruited.

Following this, another Hasdrubal, son of Gisgo, prepared his army to oppose the Romans near Carthage, placing these Celtiberians at the centre of his formation. In the ensuing battle, the African forces took to flight, but the Celtiberians held their ground until they were completely surrounded. They surrendered, and the Roman commander Publius Scipio massacred them all.

Hannibal's great adventure had now turned into a trap of his own making, and with disaster facing him on all sides he was recalled to save Carthage. In the final battle of the war, at Zama, he arranged his Celtic troops in the centre once more, along with the other mercenaries, directly behind the elephants. The Romans slowly pushed them backwards, and soon the battle developed into a mass slaughter, which Hannibal himself barely escaped with his life.

In retrospect, it can be seen that if the Celts of Italy had postponed their great contest with the Romans for a few years until the Second Punic War began, they would almost definitely have won. It was impossible for them to have such foresight, however, for the re-emergence of faraway Carthage as a super-power had come quite suddenly, and even then its attack on Rome through the Alps was unexpected. Equally unexpected, as it transpired, were the dogged persistence of the Romans and their victory over their great African rivals.

As the 2nd Century BC dawned, the whole balance of power had changed dramatically. Hannibal had come and gone, and Rome was now mistress on both sides of the Mediterranean. Much of north Africa, an increasing slice of the Greek colonies, and the Iberian Peninsula itself was under her hegemony. She reigned supreme in Italy, and the Celts had been driven back into the mountains from which they had come. The ancient sack of Rome had been duly avenged, Cisalpine Gaul had been savaged by Roman armies for more than a century, but it was not to stop there.

The city of Carthage besieged by Publius Scipio. Having taken Megara by storm, Scipio cut off the entrance to the harbour by constructing a mole across it. The Carthaginians cut a new channel to gain exit for their navy, but they were defeated by the Romans in a three-day naval battle. When the Romans made the final attack on the city, they met with fierce resistance. (From an imaginative painting by Sir E J Poynter.)

Chapter 5

STRUGGLES BY THE MEDITERRANEAN

Celtic power was on the wane, and everywhere this was due to the Romans. The Boii continued to resist in Italy, and in 200 BC they surrounded a large detachment of Roman soldiers who were cutting the corn near the fortified town of Mutilum (in the vicinity of modern Cesena). In the ensuing fighting 7,000 Roman soldiers along with their leader Gaius Ampius were slain. The fighting spread, and even the Cenomani, who had been allies of Rome in Hannibal's war, soon found that they were to get little thanks for their efforts. The Romans valued their own colonists more than erstwhile allies, and the continuing confiscation of Celtic lands in Cisalpine Gaul caused these same Cenomani to join forces with the Boii and the Insubres. The combined Celtic force numbered up to 40,000 and was aided and directed by a Carthaginian officer called Hamilcar whom Hannibal had left in Gaul. They attacked and sacked the Roman colony at Placentia, and then crossed the Po, with the intention of attacking Cremona, where the colonists quickly barricaded themselves. A large Roman force arrived to relieve the siege, and soon after they routed the Celts with great slaughter. Livy claims that more than 35,000 of the Celts were killed or captured, and Hamilcar himself was slain, as well as three of the Celtic leaders.

The Romans continued to ravage the remaining territories of the Celts in Cisalpine Gaul, and four years later the Boii hit back. A Roman army under the consul Marcus Marcellus was constructing a road through their territory, when the chieftain Corolamos attacked them with a large force and slew 3,000 of the soldiers, including several officers. Marcellus held his camp with most of his legionaries, however, and some days later he led these men in an attack on a camp of the Insubres in the region of the Comum (now Como). In furious fighting, the Roman cavalry broke the Insubres lines, and the latter took to flight. Again a huge number of Celts were slain, and 87 of their standards were taken, along with hundreds of wagons and much treasure. A necklace of great weight, which was among the booty taken by the Romans, was taken to the Capitol in Rome and presented there as a gift to the god Jupiter.

The territory of the Boii was laid waste by the Romans as far as the town of Felsina, causing the women, children, and other dependents of the Boii to retreat into the northern forests. The warriors retaliated by ravaging the lands of the Laevi and Libui, semi-Celtic tribes who were in alliance with Rome, but they unexpectedly clashed with the Romans on the borders of the Ligurian territory and were cut down almost to a man. Livy remarks that in this battle the Romans 'fought more for bloodlust than for triumph'.

The Boii were again in the field in 193 BC, in alliance with the Ligurians, who were resisting renewed Roman pressure on their lands in north-west Italy. This time they were more cautious, backing away from a Roman army under Lucius Cornelius which was plundering their territory. All the countryside was burned and looted by the Romans. The Boii waited for their opportunity for an ambush. They got it as the Romans returned to Liguria through a defile near Mutina (modern Modena), but their plan was noticed and the Romans were prepared. The Boii put the Roman front line to flight, but fresh Roman troops were introduced, bringing stalemate to the fighting. The sun blazed overhead, scorching the Boii warriors who found the excessive heat debilitating, but they stood their ground in dense formation, propping each other up as they fell. A ferocious cavalry charge by the Romans broke their lines. The Boii leaders tried to stop the disintegration, striking the backs of their terrified men with spear-shafts, but they failed to prevent a precipitous flight. The Roman cavalry cut down the terrified warriors as they fled, killing 14,000 of them and taking over a thousand prisoners. The Celts had taken their toll of the enemy also in this battle, for the Romans lost no fewer than 5,000 men, including some leading officers.

Towards the end of the same year, the Ligurians blocked a Roman army as it was going through a narrow pass in the border country of the Ligurians and Celts. The Roman commander tried to turn his army back the way they had come, but they found themselves hemmed in at the rear by a force of Celts. In these wars, the Romans had the service of Numidian cavalry which had formerly been to the fore in Hannibal's army. These Numidians now offered to relieve the situation by breaking through the Celts and going to ravage their land. The Celts were taken off guard by the pathetic appearance of these Numidians, who were poorly armed and riding scrawny, ungainly horses, and who moreover appeared to have lost control of their mounts as they approached. Drawing near, however, the Numidians changed abruptly, suddenly spurring their horses into a fierce charge, and by this ruse they broke their way through. They immediately set to burning and slaughtering all over the surrounding countryside, and the Celts had no choice but to abandon their position, each man racing to protect his own family.

In this type of fighting in their own lands, the Celts were at a great disadvantage, for the Roman armies had no scruples concerning the wholesale slaughter of villages and destruction of the countryside. The Boii made efforts to negotiate a surrender, but this was rejected, and an episode recorded for the time shows the savagery of the Roman attitude towards them. It so happened that a nobleman of the Boii went to the camp of the consul Lucius Quinctius Flaminius, with his sons, imploring the protection of the Roman people. The consul was partying with a boy-prostitute, and he enquired of the boy if he would like to see a man being killed. The boy nodded, and straight away Flaminius drew his sword and slew the unfortunate nobleman.

Preserved corpse of Gaulish warrior from Alesia, France.

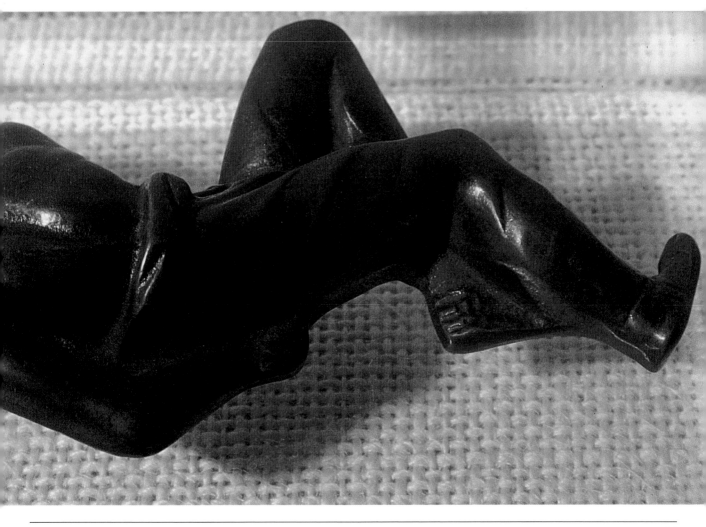

The Ligurians were defeated by the army of the proconsul Quintus Minucius in 191 BC. Incessant warfare had all but obliterated the Boii, and soon after Publius Scipio—the conqueror of Hannibal—inflicted a crushing defeat on them. They had no choice but to surrender and give hostages, after which Scipio confiscated half of their remaining lands. A great procession of triumph was held in Rome, in which prisoners, arms standards, captured horses, and booty of all kinds, were paraded through the streets in Celtic wagons. Also on display were 1,471 golden necklaces, 247 pounds weight of gold, and 2,340 pounds of silver, much of which was in the form of beautifully wrought Celtic vessels. From this time on, the Romans strictly controlled the Celts of Cisalpine Gaul, which they renamed 'Gallia Togata' (i.e., Celtdom where the Roman toga must be worn). In the year 183 BC the Roman Senate declared the Alps to be the northern border of Italy and decreed that no more Celts should cross it.

ROMANS FACE GALATIAN MERCENARIES IN THE EAST

The Romans, who had earlier gained a foothold in Illyria, on the eastern Adriatic coast, and had involved themselves on the side of the Greek states against the Macedonians, now concentrated their attention on conquests in the east. In this, their main obstacle was the humane and enlightened King Antiochus III of Syria, who had many of the Galatian Celts as mercenaries in his army, and who had given refuge to Hannibal in his court. In the year 191 BC, Antiochus crossed to Greece in support of the Macedonians, but he was defeated by the Romans a year later at the battle of Magnesia. This gave the Romans the opportunity to intervene in Asia Minor, and in the summer of 189 BC they sent an army under the command of Marcus Fulvius against the Aetolians, the result of which was the surrender of several cities to the Romans and an acceptance of their role as super-power in Asia Minor.

In that same summer, another Roman army, under Gnaeus Manlius, had established themselves at Ephesus, and was undertaking a campaign against the Galati. Addressing his soldiers, Manlius excused his aggression by saying that these Celts had supported Antiochus and, moreover, that they were by nature so ungovernable that their power must be broken. Manlius was joined in his task by an army led by Attalus, brother of the King of Pergamum, Eumenes II—both of these being sons of the old enemy of the Galati, Attalus I. The combined armies advanced in triumph north-eastwards through Asia Minor, plundering and laying heavy tribute on all the peoples in their way, until they reached Phrygia on the frontier of the territory of the Tolistoboii. 'This was the enemy with whom the Romans had now to fight,' states Livy, 'an enemy very terrifying to all the people of that region.'

Manlius again addressed his soldiers rhetorically, calling the Celts 'a fierce nation' and stating that they ranked highest of all the peoples of Asia Minor in their reputation for war. He went on: 'Their tall physique, their flowing red hair, their huge shields and enormous swords, along with their songs as they go into battle, their howling and leaping, and the fearful din of arms as they bang their shields according to some kind of ancestral custom—all these things are designed to terrify!' Then Manlius gave a long lecture on the history of the Celts in Italy, and on how the Romans alone had never feared them but had repeatedly defeated them in battle. He compared the Galati to wild animals, whose fathers and grandfathers had been been 'driven from their land by the barrenness of the soil' and had made their way through Illyricum, Paenoia, and Thrace, being 'hardened and made savage by all their misfortunes'. In Asia Minor, however, they had been tamed and softened by the rich lifestyle there. So the celebrated 'Celtic frenzy' in battle should not be feared, and Manlius here gave the typical Roman strategic assessment of Celtic warriors:

> *This has been learned from experience—that if you withstand the first charge, into which they hurl themselves with blazing passion and blind rage, their limbs become slack with sweat and weariness, their weapons waver in their hands. They are flabby in body, flabby in resolve when their passion subsides, and they are laid low by sun, dust, and thirst, so that you need not even use weapons against them then.*

Despite his confident attitude, Manlius took care to contact one of the Galatian leaders, Eposognatos, who had refused to support Antiochus against the Romans. This Episognatos was one of the leading men of the Tectosages, and he concluded a treaty of friendship with Manlius, who then proceeded to encamp near Cuballum, a

Model of a Gaulish warrior, France, period not known. Note the oblong shield and the scabbard below it. The warrior also appears to be wearing leggings.

stronghold of the Tolistoboii. A sudden attack was made on the camp by Galatian cavalry, which retreated after inflicting some casualties on the Romans. Next day Manlius moved on to Gordium (in the centre of modern Turkey), where Episognatus contacted him with news that he had failed to get the other leaders of the Galati to join his alliance with the Romans, and that the vast bulk of the Tolistoboii under their chieftain Ortiago was moving to Mount Olympus (just north of Göynük), bringing their families and herds with them in the hope of resisting the Roman army from that position. It was later reported that the Tectosages, under Combilomaros, had gone to fortify themselves further east on Mount Magaba; and that the Trocmi, having left their dependents with these Tectosages, were going with their chieftain Gaulotos to join the Tolistoboii..

Confident that the Romans would be sufficiently weakened by the ascent of the steep and freezing Mount Olympus, the Tolistoboii threw a ditch and other defensive works around the summit. Encamping within 5 miles (8km) of the mountain, Manlius made sure that he had a sufficient amount of missiles and javelins to undertake an assault. He then went with Attalus and 400 cavalrymen to reconnoitre, but was attacked by the Galatian cavalry and put to flight. Some days later he set out again to reconnoitre, this time with his whole force. He discovered a route running to the summit and decided that the main prong of his attack would be from there. Sending two smaller contingents by more difficult routes, and leaving his cavalry and elephants on level ground at the foot of the mountain, he commenced the ascent. The Galati,

Celtic leader in chariot. Detail from terracotta frieze in the temple at Civita Alba, near Sassoferrato in eastern Italy. Now at Museo Civica, Bologna.

suspecting an assault only from the facile path, sent about 4,000 warriors to occupy a hill there.

This hill was the first objective of the Romans' advance. They discharged volleys of missiles, arrows, and javelins at the Galati, who were equipped only for fighting at close quarters with swords. The frustrated Galati had only stones to throw back, as they were struck by a mass of missiles. They fought naked, and with their shields not large enough to cover their bodies. The sight of the gashes, and of the red and blackened blood flowing from their white bodies, was horrible, but they attempted to cut the javelins and arrows from their own flesh, imagining that the terrible wounds brought them greater glory. They rushed madly at the Romans, who used their short swords with deadly effect at close range. Most of this Galatian force was slaughtered, and the remainder raced back up the mountain to their women and children, who were in a state of absolute panic. As the main body of the Romans advanced, the two other contingents joined them, and the whole force prepared to attack the summit.

The Galati had taken up position in front of their final rampart near the summit, and they were overwhelmed by missiles of all kinds and were driven back behind the rampart. Then the Romans unleashed a torrent of missiles right into the Galatian camp, where men, women, and children were crowded in a panic. The Romans knew by the shouting of the warriors, and the wailing of the women and children, that the missiles had had deadly effect; and soon the legionaries burst into the camp itself. The whole crowd of the Galati took to flight, running headlong down the steep mountain slopes, and being massacred by the pursuing Romans as they went. Manlius ordered his men to kill as many as possible of the fugitives, and those fortunate enough to reach the foot of the mountains encountered the Roman cavalry, who wrought further havoc on them. In all, about 10,000 people were slain, and about 30,000 were taken prisoner.

Manlius now set out to destroy the Tectosages, and after a three-day march he reached Ancyra (modern Ankara), about 10 miles (16km) from their fortifications on Mount Magaba. He had brought a huge number of captives with him, among whom was Chiomara, wife of the Tolistoboii chieftain Ortiago. She was a very beautiful woman, and the centurion in charge of her detachment tried to seduce her and, failing this, raped her. Greed was added to his lust, for the centurion then offered her freedom in return for a large ransom in gold. Desiring to keep knowledge of this from his soldiers, he made arrangements secretly to bring her to an appointed place outside the camp and to trade her to her own people for the gold. Chiomara accepted this arrangement, but when they reached the place and the gold was being paid out by her people, she ordered them 'in her own language to draw their swords and kill the centurion as he was weighing his money'. They cut his throat and decapitated him, and Chiomara wrapped his head in her garment and brought it to her husband. She threw it at his feet, explaining to him that 'there is only one man alive who has partaken of my bed!'

Meanwhile, the Tectosages sent envoys to Manlius offering peace, and a meeting was arranged halfway between the Roman camp at Ancyra and the Galatian camp on Mount Magaba. Manlius went to the rendezvous, accompanied by 500 cavalry, but found no-one there. The same envoys turned up again at the Roman camp, explaining that their chieftains could not come on account of a religious obstacle, but that they would send delegates to another meeting. After further procrastination, Manlius realised that the Galati were playing for time in order to get their dependents and valuables away from the area. Finally, the Galati

ambushed the consul with a large force of cavalry as he was proceeding to a meeting. They routed his strong bodyguard, and would have captured him if a force of Roman foragers had not come to his rescue. Most of the Galatian ambushers were put to death by the Romans for their breach of faith.

The Romans, burning with anger at this episode, prepared for an all-out assault on Mount Magaba. About 50,000 fighters of the Tectosages and Trocmi prepared for the defence, but the legionaries — using the same tactics as at Mount Olympus—routed them. Thousands of the Galati were slain, but most of the Roman soldiers stopped at their camp, attracted by the huge amount of plunder there. This allowed the greater part by far of the Galati to escape, and these later sued for peace and agreed to send envoys to discuss surrender. Manlius was confident that his conquest was complete and realised that winter was approaching and that he would soon be isolated in the coldness of the mountains. He was therefore in a hurry to return to Ephesus, and directed the Tectosages and Trocmi to send the envoys to him there. The Romans were by now in control of all of Asia Minor, and the Galati—having lost their independence—were much reduced. Many of them were in slavery, and those who remained in their own lands were placed under the rule of Rome's ally, King Eumenes II of Pergamum.

Despite all this, the Galati made a remarkable recovery. First of all, the Tolistoboii leader, Ortagio, strove to unite the three tribes and so assert their independence. Polybius describes

Gallia, the land of Gaul, represented as a woman. Female personification of the earth was common among ancient peoples, including the Celts, and this head was probably understood as that of a goddess. From a coin now in a museum in Rome.

Ortagio thus: 'He possessed many qualities, which he owed to his natural gifts and to acquired experience. He was generous and magnanimous, affable and prudent in dealing with people and — what matters most among the Galati—he was brave and skilled in the affairs of war.' Ortagio managed to forge an alliance with King Prusias of Bithynia and King Pharnakes of Pontus against King Eumenes, an arrangement which looked promising for a while but which ended in Pharnakes assuming control of the Galati and garrisoning their territory. Shocked by his cruelty, the Galati appealed for help to Eumenes.

Ortagio seems to have died by this time, and the Galati were led by two chieftains, Cassignatos and Gaizatorix. By the year 179 BC they had succeeded in driving Pharnakes out of their territories, but were displeased enough with Eumenes to forge a new alliance with Prusias against him. In 167 BC, under the chieftain Advertas, they over-ran Pergamum and almost overthrew Eumenes, but the Romans intervened to resolve the issue. Two years later it was agreed that the Galati should withdraw from Pergamum but that Eumenes should accept their independence. Henceforth, however, the Galati, in common with all the peoples of the Balkans and Asia Minor, were dependent on the Roman Senate as ultimate arbiter in their territorial and other disputes.

BELOW RIGHT: Italian representation of a barbarian woman, probably a Celt. The simplicity is in sharp contrast to the more formal depictions of Roman women.

Meanwhile, in Iberia, the ending of the Second Punic War had not brought peace. The Romans, taking the place of the Carthaginians as overlords, divided the whole peninsula into two regions—which they called 'Hispania Citerior' (Hither Spain) and 'Hispania Ulterior' (Further Spain)—and proceeded to levy taxes on all the peoples there. This led in 197 BC to an uprising in Hither Spain by the Turdetani—neighbours and close associates of the Celtiberi—and they routed a Roman army under the proconsul Gaius Sempronius, slaying many Roman officers including Sempronius himself. After a defeat near their town of Turda, the Turdetani continued the struggle and hired 10,000 fighters of the Celtiberi for this purpose. The disaffection spread, and the Romans began to disarm the Iberians, stating blandly that this was for their own protection from the hazards of war. In 195 BC, the notoriously severe consul Marcus Porcius Cato was sent by sea to pacify the Peninsula, and he began by trying to buy off the Celtiberi. One report is that they demanded two hundred talents as the price of their support, and that he saw no choice in the matter but to agree. In the space of little more than a year, he had taken many towns and seized the silver and gold mines of eastern Spain, but he was removed at the instigation of his rival Publius Scipio.

Sporadic fighting continued in the Iberian Peninsula for several years, with Scipio conquering more and more territory. Once Cato had departed, the Celtiberi returned to the road of rebellion, and in the winter of 193 BC a combined force of Vaccaei, Vettones, and Celtiberi was defeated near the town of Toletum (Toledo) by Gaius Flaminius, and their king, Hilernus, was captured. Things were quiet for a while, but a Roman plan to bring thousands of settlers to the Peninsula caused great anxiety among the Celtiberi, and in 181 BC they mustered a huge force—about 35,000 men—to oppose the Roman proconsul Quintus Fulvius Flaccus. At the beginning of spring in that year, the two armies were within a few miles of each other near the town of Aebura (now Talavera). The Celtiberi drew up their line halfway between the two camps, on a level plain, while the Romans remained in their fortified camp.

For four days the positions remained so, until the Romans suddenly sent a force by night to a hill at the rear of the Celtiberi, while another force advanced straight towards them from the front. The cavalry and infantry of the Celtiberi advanced to meet the latter force. When they had thus proceeded far from their camp, the Romans on the hill attacked the camp and set it on fire. The two armies had come into contact and the fighting had begun, when the Celtiberi noticed what had happened. They wavered for a short while between returning to save the camp or continuing the battle, and this was enough to give the advantage to the Romans. After a stubborn fight, the Celtiberi were surrounded, and over 20,000 of them were killed and almost 5,000 captured, along with 500 horses. The Romans lost almost 4,000 men.

Sculpture from a sepulchre at Florence, Italy. In relief on the side of the sepulchre, the Roman nbobleman is represented as triumphant over Celtic warriors: the scene includes the depiction of a Roman cavalryman spearing a fallen Celt.

The Romans followed up this victory by advancing towards the Celtic town of Contrebia (modern Botorrita, near Zaragoza), which surrendered. A Celtiberian force, which had been delayed by heavy rain and floods, came to the assistance of the town. Seeing no signs of Romans there, they approached in disarray and without any precautions. Suddenly the Romans sallied forth, and again the Celtiberi were routed, with thousands slain. The survivors returned to their homes and villages, while Flaccus took his legions throughout the whole countryside, plundering as they went. As he took fortress after fortress, the great majority of the Celtiberi surrendered to him.

Having cowed the defeated Celtiberi by parading his large army through their territories, Flaccus in the following spring began to ravage the lands of the tribes of the interior, who had not yet surrendered. In retaliation these tribes ambushed his legions at the Manlian Pass, in the Sistema Berico mountains where the Celtic Berones had their territory. The fighting was fierce, and the Celtiberi used a wedge formation to try to break the Roman lines. Flaccus ordered his cavalry to give their horses their heads in order to give more force to their attack on the wedge. The tactic succeeded, and the Celtiberi were put to flight with great slaughter. Their warriors were cut down by the pursuing Romans all along the pass, about 17,000 being slain and 3,700 captured along with 600 horses.

In179 BC the two praetors Sempronius Gracchus and Postumius Albinus undertook to finally crush the Vaccaei and Celtiberi, and it is reported that in their campaign they destroyed no fewer than 300 fortresses. On one occasion, when he was besieging the Celtiberian town of Certina, Gracchus had an experience which brought home to him the differences in attitude between the Celts and the Romans. A deputation came to him from the town, saying that they intended to fight and seeking his permission to go and consult with their people in the countryside. Gracchus and his officers were amazed at this old-world heroic attitude to war, but permission was granted. The envoys returned from their business a few days later, and since it was midday they demanded a drink before they spoke. Then they demanded a second drink, much to the amusement of the Roman bystanders, and finally enquired of the Romans by what means they intended to take the town. Gracchus replied that he would do so by relying on his army, which was of exceptional quality, and had his soldiers paraded before them in order to impress the truth of this on them. The envoys departed, and soon after the town surrendered.

These envoys had gone to consult with the Celtiberian force which was encamped at the town of Alce (modern Alcázar), and Gracchus lost no time in going there. He had his men engage in several minor actions against that force, to give them false confidence and thereby to draw them gradually out of their camp. Finally, he made a mock attack on the Celtiberi, instructing his men to retreat towards their own camp as if under strong pressure. The ruse succeeded, for the whole Celtiberi force rushed headlong into the Roman camp, only to find themselves confronted by a far superior force. The Celtiberian camp was ultimately taken, and 9,000 of them slain, to the loss of 109 on the Roman side. After this battle, Gracchus ordered his troops to devastate Celtiberia. They took a huge amount of plunder, as well as many noblemen as prisoners. Among these was the Celtiberian chieftain Thurrus, regarded by the Romans as the most influential man in Spain. Thurrus agreed to change sides, on the condition that his life and that of his children were spared, and he afterwards served successfully as a Roman army officer.

When the stronghold of Ergavica fell to the Romans, the power of the Celtiberi was almost at an end, but they made one last effort. In the Chaunus mountains (near modern Complega), they fought a pitched battle with the legions of Gracchus, which lasted from daybreak to the sixth hour, with great losses on both sides. The Romans were reeling from this surprise result, but with characteristic resilience they returned to harass the Celtiberian camp next day. On the third day, the Celtiberi emerged from their camp, but were defeated by the Romans with the loss of over 20,000 men. The enormous losses suffered by the Celtiberi in this whole war meant that they were in no position to assert their power or even their rights from that time on. Gracchus's word was law, and he set about dismantling the whole social structure of Celtiberia by establishing Roman towns in their lands and by encouraging Celtiberian warriors to enlist in the Roman army.

He did, however, introduce a more reasonable taxation system, and his stern combination of conquest and diplomacy resulted in 20 years more or less free of fighting. The only exception was when, some years after his departure, the Celtiberi made a surprise attack on the camp of the new praetor Appius Claudius. The attack was unsuccessful, with the Celtiberi again losing thousands of men, but the fact that it was attempted in itself shows both the relief at the departure of so ruthless a Roman leader and also the abiding hope of the Celtiberi that they could one day muster a force which would expel the Romans.

CELTIBERIANS IN REVOLT SCORE VICTORIES OVER ROMANS

They tried again in 153 BC, when two of their tribes, the Belli and Titti, joined a revolt of the Lusitani. They began by adding to the fortifications of Segeda (modern Seges), which was in breach of the treaty with Gracchus. The rebels had a charismatic leader called Salendicos, who brandished a silver spear and claimed that it had been sent to him from heaven. He prophesied victory for his people, and his courage matched his vision, for he tried to assassinate the consul. Entering the camp by night, he managed to get quite near to the consul's tent before he was speared to death by a sentinel. The Romans were so alarmed at the situation that they brought the date of the New Year forward from March 15 to January 1, an alteration which became the basis for the Calendar which is still in use today. This facilitated the appointment of a new consul specifically for the task of suppressing the revolt, and this consul—Fulvius Nobilior—soon set out with an army of 30,000 men, with ten elephants and a force of Numidian cavalry in support. He destroyed the town of Segeda, but the inhabitants had already fled to join their compatriots in the great hill-fort of Numantia (to the north of modern Garray in Soria). In expectation of a Roman attack, the Celtiberi chose Ambro and Leuco as their leaders.

Nobilior now besieged that fortress, and the Celtiberi showered rocks onto the attackers. One of the elephants was struck, and it caused the others to panic. Many of the soldiers were trampled and, seeing the confusion, the Celtiberi surged down from the hill-fort and put the whole Roman force to flight. Soon after, they appointed a new leader, called Carus, who had a reputation for military skill. Three days after his election, he placed 20,000 horse and 5,000 foot soldiers in ambush in a dense forest and atacked the Roman army as it passed by. The Celtiberi scored a great victory, with 6,000 of the Romans slain. Carus led a pursuit of the fleeing soldiers, but he was counter-attacked by the Roman cavalry who were guarding the

Another series of figures in relief on a Roman tomb in Florence. Note the round shields of the defeated warriors, indicating that they were Celts.

baggage. In the ensuing struggle, thousands of his men were slain, and he himself, although 'performing prodigies of valour', also fell.

In 152 BC Nobilior was succeeded as governor of Hither Spain by Claudius Marcellus, who besieged Ocilis, a town of the Nergobriges, a Celtiberian tribe who lived near Zaragoza. Fearing defeat, the Nergobriges sent a delegate 'who wore a wolf's skin instead of bearing a herald's staff, and begged forgiveness'. Marcellus replied that he would not grant this unless all the Arevaci, Belli, and Titti would ask for it together. Accordingly, when Marcellus besieged the fortress of Numantia, the new Arevaci leader Litenno came out of the fortress and held a conference with him. Marcellus warned that a tough Roman leader, Lucius Licinius Lucullus, was being sent to reduce the Celtiberi and their allies, and as a result Litenno surrendered to him on behalf of all the tribes.

Marcellus had saved the Celtiberi from the brutality of Lucullus, who began his campaign in 151 BC with the massacre of the Vaccaei in northern Spain. He then moved south to join the governor of Further Spain, Servius Sulpicius Galba, in the war against the Lusitani, who had inflicted a heavy defeat on the latter. Soon after, Lucullus and Galba caught the Lusitani in a pincer movement, and the latter surrendered. Galba pretended to be lenient, but then treacherously surrounded the Lusitani and sent in soldiers to slaughter them 'as they lamented and invoked the names of the gods and the pledges which they had received'. In these and other massacres, Galba mercilessly slew 9,000 of the Lusitani, and sold 20,000 into slavery.

One of the survivors of the massacres was a young man with the Celtic name of Viriathos. He had started life as a shepherd and hunter, then turned to banditry, and finally became the leader of the Lusitani in their efforts to reverse their fortune. A skilled horseman and swordsman, Viriathos soon showed his talent and resourcefulness, luring the Romans into ambushes, and bringing fire and sword to all their possessions on both banks of the Ibero and Tagus. He defeated Roman armies under various generals, but his most celebrated triumph was gained over Caius Vettilius at Tribola, south of Osuna in the extreme south of the Peninsula. Here he feigned flight, thereby leading the Romans into a dense thicket, where they were ambushed and 10,000 of them were slain. After these victories, he erected—in the mountains of Lusitania—trophies adorned with robes and fasces taken from the Roman commanders.

To relieve Roman pressure on the Lusitani, Viriathos managed to persuade the Celtic and

semi-Celtic tribes of Arevaci, Belli and Titti to join his revolt in 143 BC. In response, the consul Quintus Caecilius Metellus was sent to attack Celtiberia with a large army, and he took the hill-forts of Nertobriga, Centrobriga (modern Ricla) and Contrebia (modern Botorrita). His successor as consul, Quintus Pompeius Aulus, attacked Numantia two years later, but his forces were routed by the 8,000 Celtiberian defenders there. After further setbacks, he agreed to a peace treaty with the Celtiberi, but soon after he broke the treaty and began hostilities again.

Another Roman army was sent in 142 BC to crush the Lusitanian revolt. It was under the command of the consul Fabius Maximus, but Viriathos trapped this army at Erisana (now Azuagia) and forced Fabius to agree to a treaty. According to this, the territory occupied by the Lusitani was to be left under their control and Viriathos was to be recognised as 'a friend of the Roman nation'. The outraged Roman Senate had no choice but to ratify the treaty, but they were determined to find a way around it. Thus, in 140 BC Servus Caepio was sent to Spain with a strong army, and he drove Viriathos's forces back into Lusitania and cut them off from the support of all their allies. In these straits, Viriathos offered fresh negotiations, which Caepio pretended to accept. Viriathos sent three of his most trusted friends, Audax, Ditalco, and Minuvius, to negotiate, but Caepio bribed them to assassinate their leader. Soon after, while

Dying Gaulish warrior, from the temple frieze at Civita Alba near Sassoferrato in eastern Italy. Now in Museo Civico, Bologna.

Viriathos was sleeping, these three stabbed him in the throat and slew him. The Roman writer Florus says that, in this way, although overcome, Viriathos gained 'the glory of seeming to have been invincible by any other means'. The respects paid to him by his followers are described thus by the historian Appian:

> They arranged the body of Viriathos in splendid garments and burned it on a lofty funeral pile. Many sacrifices were offered for him. The infantry and cavalry ran in troops around him, in armour, singing his praises in barbarian fashion, and they all sat around the pyre until the fire had gone out. When the obsequies were ended, they held contests in swordsmanship at his tomb.

The Romans now clearly had the upper hand, but the Lusitani and Celtiberi continued to resist. In 138 BC, a large Roman army under the general Mancinus besieged Numantia but, failing to take it and running short of supplies, decided to evacuate by night. The Celtiberi rushed out from their fort to attack the retreating Romans, and the fighting turned into a rout, with thousands of Romans surrendering. Mancinus made a truce with the Celtiberi, but this was rejected by the Roman Senate, who were livid that he had allowed his army of 30,000 soldiers to be defeated by a force of 4,000 Celtiberi. On his own request, the disgraced Mancinus was handed over naked to the Celtiberi, but they—probably realising that he had acted in good faith—refused to take him as a prisoner.

CELTIBERI BESIEGED AT HILL-FORTRESS OF NUMANTIA

The Romans now sent one of their best commanders, Scipio Aemilianus (adopted son of the celebrated Publius Scipio), with 60,000 men to pursue the war, and he laid siege to the great hill-fortress of Numantia, which was being held by Avaros, the Celtiberian leader. Scipio surrounded the town with ballistas and catapults, and several attempts by Avaros's men to dislodge the Romans from their positions failed. These attacks were fierce, and accompanied by great commotion and trumpet-blowing, but the besiegers held firm. Finally the Celtiberi began to run out of supplies, and a chieftain named Rhetogenes Caraunios was chosen to attempt to break through the Roman lines with a few men. This small group slipped out of Numantia under cover of darkness, slew the Roman sentries, and scaled the siege-works with a folding ladder. Reaching a neighbouring hill-fort, Rhetogenes appealed to the Arevaci there to come to the assistance of Avaros, but they had gone into alliance with the Romans and refused. At Lutia 400 young men agreed to join Rhetogenes, but the older and more cautious citizens of that town sent word of what was happening to Scipio. He immediately sent a legion to besiege Lutia, and under threat of massacre the town surrendered. Scipio had the young rebels paraded before him and ordered their right hands to be cut off.

Meanwhile, the besieged Celtiberi at Numantia were being reduced to starvation and even cannibalism. Rumour spread that Avaros and his family had made a secret deal with the Romans, and as a result Avaros was assassinated and the defenders surrendered. The Latin writer Appian — drawing on a lost account by Polybius — describes their state:

> First of all, those who wished to do so killed themselves in various ways. Then the rest went out on the third day to the appointed place, a strange and shocking spectacle. Their bodies were foul, their hair and nails long, and they were smeared with filth. They smelt most horribly, and the clothes they wore were likewise squalid and emitted an equally foul odour. For these reasons they appeared pitiable to their enemies, but at the same time there was something fearful in the expression of their eyes—an expression of anger, pain and weariness, and the awareness of having eaten human flesh..

Fifty warriors were selected by Scipio to grace his triumphant march through Rome, and the rest were sold into slavery, while the great hill-fort of Numantia itself was burned and razed to the ground. For the next 50 years the Celtiberi were brutally held down by Roman commanders, and various minor rebellions were crushed without mercy. As Europe underwent vast changes in the final century before Christ, Celtiberian independence was a thing of the past, and the Celtic language and culture in the Peninsula began to disappear along with most of the other languages and cultures in the increasingly Latinised south-west corner of the European Continent.

Chapter 6

THE COLLAPSE OF GAUL

Rome was now in a position to extend its influence permanently north of the Alps, and an occasion for this presented itself in the year 154 BC when the Salluvii, a mixed tribe of Celts and Ligurians, launched an attack on the Greek colony of Marseilles. The assault was repulsed by the Massiliotes with the help of Roman troops, but the Salluvii returned to the attack in 125 BC, and now the Romans offered—under guise of protection—to control all the Massiliote territory, which stretched from Cisalpine Gaul along the coast to Marseilles. This was accepted, and the consul Fulvius Flaccus defeated the Saluvii in battle. Some of their leaders fled northwards to take refuge with the powerful Celtic tribe, the Allobroges, who were allied to the even more powerful Arverni in the Rhône valley. The Arverni had for some generations been the leading Celtic group in that whole area. Their king Bituitis was a son of the former king Lovernios (literally 'the fox'), who was famed for his lavishness. The following is an account of Lovernios given by the writer Athenaeus, quoting Posidonius:

In an attempt to win popular favour he rode in a chariot over the plains, distributing gold and silver to the tens of thousands of Celts who followed him. Moreover, he made a square enclosure one and a half miles each way, within which he filled vats with expensive liquor, and prepared so great a quantity of food that for many days all who wished could enter and enjoy the prepared feast, it being served without a break by the attendants. And when at length he fixed a day for the ending of the feast, a Celtic poet, who arrived too late, met Lovernios and composed a song magnifying his greatness and regretting his own late arrival. Lovernios was very pleased, and asked for a bag of gold and threw it to the poet who ran beside his chariot. The poet picked it up and sang another song, saying that the very tracks made by his chariot on the earth gave gold and largesse to mankind.

The Romans were of course very anxious to reduce and loot a kingdom which had such a reputation for wealth, and they used the issue of the Salluvii refugees as a pretext for launching an all-out campaign against both the Allobroges and Arverni. Two strong armies were accordingly sent northwards under Domitius Ahenobarbus and Fabius Maximus in 121 BC. The combined Roman armies clashed with a force of 20,000 Arverni warriors at

ABOVE *Neat remains of a Roman village at Bories, in Provence, a region which served as the base for Roman operations in Gaul.*

LEFT: *Celtic charioteer in action at the battle of Vindalum, in which Bituitis, king of the Arverni, was defeated by the Romans. The figure may represent Bituitis himself in his silver chariot. From a Roman denarius found in Narbonne, in the south of France. Now at Cabinet des Medailles, Biblioth`eque Nationale, Paris.*

Vindalum (where the river Sorgue flows into the Rhône). The king of the Arverni, Bituitis—flambuoyant like his father—was a conspicuous figure in the battle as he wore variegated armour and drove a silver chariot. It is further reported that he was surprised that the Romans did not have as large a force as his and that he boasted that they would 'hardly suffice to feed the dogs which he had in his army'.

When the fighting began, however, his army was dispirited by the sight of elephants in the Roman army, 'which matched the fierceness of these people', and the Arverni were routed. Bituitis had many boats chained together so as to ferry his men across the Rhône, and in their haste to retreat the chains broke, causing as many to be drowned as were slain. While Fabius ravaged the territory of the Allobroges, Ahenobarbus forced other tribes of the area, such as the Helvetii and the section of the Tectosages who inhabited Toulouse, to conclude treaties of 'friendship' with Rome. Bituitis, who had survived the battle of Vindalum, also offered to make peace with Rome, stating that he wished to deal with the Roman Senate in person. Once he arrived in Italy, however, he and his son Congentiatos were detained by the Romans as virtual prisoners.

The Romans celebrated their first triumph in Transalpine Gaul by founding a colony at Narbonne and naming the whole area as the province of 'Gallia Narbonensis', from which comes the designation Provence. They also built a great road stretching all the way from Genoa to there, and further along the eastern coast of Spain as far as Cartagena. Celtic and other peoples inhabiting that whole area soon came to terms with the new arrangements, and had little choice but to offer themselves as allies to the new superpower. Among these were the strong Celtic tribe of the northern Rhône valley, the Aedui, and this particular alliance gave the Romans a hand in affairs at the very heart of Celtic territory.

Before the Romans could extend their power further, however, a new threat emerged from the north. The Cimbri and Teutones were Germanic peoples who had originated in the area of the North Sea and had been encroaching on Celtic territories for some time. During the course of their expansion, these people—and particularly the Cimbri—seem to have absorbed a good deal of Celtic influence, so that many of their recorded leaders were known by Celtic or Celticised names. The Romans were confused as to their exact identity, and sometimes in fact equated them with the more northernly Celts. At any rate, the Cimbri began first to exert pressure on the Boii, Volcae Tectosages, and Taurisci of southern Germany and northern Austria. They advanced west as far as the Rhine and south as far as the Danube, and the Celtic peoples in these areas were either pushed before them—like the Helvetii—or gradually merged with them. The Romans, alarmed at the prospect of such a potent new force, sent an army under the consul Papirius Carbo in 113 BC to oppose them, but this army was defeated near the headquarters of the Taurisci at Noreia (modern Magdalenenburg).

In the year 111 BC the Cimbri spread westwards, into the Rhône Valley, and began to threaten the province of Gallia Narbonensis. The Roman governor of the province, Junius Silanus, refused their offers of negotiation and attacked them, but his army was routed. The Cimbri, under Claodicus, were now joined by the Teutones under their leader Teutobodunos, and by Celtic tribes of the area. The Tectosages also rebelled and laid siege to the Roman garrison at Toulouse in 107 BC. They were joined by the Tigurini, a branch of the Helvetii. To counter this, the Romans sent two new armies into Gaul, under the consuls Lucius Cassius Longinus and Servilius Caepio. Longinus chased the Tigurini north-west through the Garonne Valley as far as the territory of the Nitiobriges, and there—near Agen—the Tigurini made a stand under their leader Divico. The Romans were defeated, and Longinus himself was slain.

Meanwhile, the army of Caepio managed to relieve the siege of Toulouse and inflicted a defeat on the Tectosages, who surrendered. Caepio, knowing that the Gauls were accustomed to load their temples with offerings, seized a huge amount of gold there. Some accounts claim that he took the gold from a sacred lake near Toulouse, and that this gold was the treasure which the Tectosages had seized at Delphi almost two hundred years before. Caepio tried

Roman victory arch at Orange, commemorating the triumph of the legions over the Germanic tribes, the Teutones and Cimbri, and their Celtic allies, in the great war of 113-101 BC. Orange itself had been the site of a crushing defeat of a Roman army in the course of the war.

to keep the treasure for himself, but was later accused of purloining it from the Roman State. His victory at Toulouse proved to be a hollow one, for within two years another Roman army was wiped out at Orange, and a combined force of Cimbri and Teutones then proceeded to cross the Pyrenees and enter Spain. They met with stout resistance there from the Roman garrisons, helped by Celtiberian tribes who had no welcome for more strangers in search of land. This contingent soon returned from Spain and joined their main force which was now threatening Italy itself.

In 102 BC it was only with great difficulty that the Cimbri were prevented from going through the Brenner Pass by a large Roman army. Soon after, the Teutones were defeated with great slaughter by Gaius Marius as they attempted to enter Italy from the direction of Gallia Narbonensis. A few surviving horsemen took refuge with the Celtic Sequani, but the Sequani were forced by the Romans to hand them over for execution. Finally, in 101 BC, the Cimbri broke through into Italy with an enormous force, and the advancing horde was confronted by the Romans under Marius near Vercellae, between Milan and Turin. It was a very hot day, and the adroit Marius had his soldiers advance through the dust and haze. To the consternation of the Cimbri, the Romans suddenly charged upon them from the east, with their helmets seeming to be on fire from the shining of the sun's rays. In a ferocious struggle, the Cimbri were defeated, and it is reported that no fewer than 60,000 of their fighters were killed. Boiorix, a man with a Celtic name who was the leader of the Cimbri in this battle, fell, fighting furiously and slaying many of his opponents. The Roman writers claimed that the women and children of the Cimbri, who had been taken with them in wagons, then proceeded to commit suicide, but we can be sure that the Romans themselves had a hand in the indiscriminate slaughter which followed.

CELTS JOIN SPARTACUS IN REVOLT

The power of the Cimbri and Teutones had been broken even more abruptly than it had arisen, but as a result of the great battles fought a huge number of captives had been taken by the Romans, and this swelled the slave population of Rome. Many of the slaves who joined the revolt of the gladiator Spartacus in 73 BC were Cimbri, Teutones, and Celts. Spartacus himself was a Thracian and two of his generals, Crixos and Cenomaros, had Celtic names. Indeed, during his revolt, Spartacus got large numbers of recruits from Cisalpine Gaul and, when he was defeated two years later by a large Roman army under Marcus Licinius Crassus, the thousands of his men who were crucified between Capua and Rome must have included many Celtic warriors who had risked all in his daring adventure for freedom.

Everywhere, it was the Roman power which now was crucial to the Celts, and their history was being reshaped in the context of struggles which were developing within the Roman world itself. The first such power-struggle was between Gaius Marius and another famous general, Lucius Cornelius Sulla. Marius represented the popular party and Sulla the nobility. The struggle continued for 30 years and outlasted the deaths of both leaders. Many of the leading figures used the Celtic world as their stamping-ground and as the arena for gaining credit at home.

Iberia was a clear instance, where, in 83 BC, a Roman governor—Quintus Sertorius, who belonged to the popular party in Rome—was assigned to Spain. In the following year Sulla had himself appointed dictator, and Sertorius joined the Lusitani in a revolt. Many of the other leading tribes flocked to his support, including the Celtiberi, Vaccaei, and Vettones. Although a brilliant strategist, Sertorius was also something of a charlatan, and he inspired religious awe in his Iberian supporters by claiming that his pet white fawn was an intermediary between himself and the gods. He succeeded in holding Spain against the Roman armies sent there, including one led by the celebrated Pompeius Cneus (Pompey) in 77 BC, but was assassinated four years later by his lieutenent Perpenna.

The Peninsula was relatively quiet when an ambitious young Roman named Caius Julius Caesar was appointed as quaestor in Further Spain in 68 BC. He was connected by marriage to Marius, and therefore belonged to the same party as Sertorius. Caesar, however, was far more ambitious and destined for a far more successful career. His first tour of duty in Spain disappointed him, since it offered no opportunity for glory, and he soon returned to Italy. There he flung himself headlong into the factionalism between various groups who were contending for power. His political skills became clear when a conspiracy was discovered by the orator Cicero in 63 BC. The conspiracy was organised by a Roman nobleman, Sergius Catilina, who

planned to assassinate the upper class senators and confiscate their wealth. A delegation was in Rome at the time from the Allobroges, one of the Celtic peoples in Transalpine Gaul, who were complaining about the way in which Roman governors were plundering their tribe. Catilina contacted these envoys and, on hearing of their determination to be rid of the rapacity of the Romans, he enlisted them into his group. Feeling insecure in the confines of Rome and its internal squabbles, however, the Allobroges decided that it would be safer for them to inform Cicero, and this they did. Cicero quickly used them as agents to gain more information on the conspiracy, and thus had Catilina and his followers arrested. Suspicion of involvement in the conspiracy fell on Caesar also, but he had so ingratiated himself with the people by lavish games and entertainments that he survived.

The Lusitani embarked on a series of raids again in the Iberian Pensinsula, and this led directly to the appointment in 62 BC of Caesar as governor of Further Spain. He was now determined to use the opportunity to further his political ambitions at home, and also to gain enough wealth to clear the massive debts which he had incurred. An anecdote told of his journey to Spain illustrates the manner in which he intended to use the Celts. Passing through a miserable little Alpine village, his companions remarked that people in that place were as ambitious as those in any other place, whereupon Caesar answered that he himself would prefer to be 'the first man here than the second in Rome'. Eager for glory and to emulate the achievements of other Roman commanders, he began by leading a military campaign against the Lusitani. He won several battles, establishing his authority as far as the Atlantic, and then sailed up along the coast and took the Celtiberian city of Brigantium (modern La Coruña) in the north.

He returned hastily to Rome in 60 BC to contend for the consulship, which he gained, and then courted the friendship of the two leading figures, Crassus and Pompey, although these two were rivals to each other. The end result was a general reconciliation of the three men, and the establishment in 59 BC of a triumvirate by which they ruled the Empire together. Caesar next achieved two of his principal purposes—one was the reduction of the power of Cicero, and the other was having himself put in charge of the Roman province of Gaul for five years. This latter office he intended as a springboard to total power in Rome.

By this time, the Celtic world was under great pressure, and this reflected itself in civil wars between the inhabitants of Transalpine Gaul. The Aedui had begun to challenge the weakened Arverni and their allies the Sequani, and around 70 BC these two latter tribes had brought in some Germanic mercenaries to assist them. The result was that the king of the Germanic Suebi, Ariovistus, got a foothold among the Sequani, who came more and more under his control. The Aedui mustered as many of their neighbours as they could, and spearheaded the resistance against Ariovistus. In 61 BC, however, Ariovistus scored a massive victory over a united force of several Celtic tribes at Admagetobriga (in Alscace), after which he began to penetrate further into the Celtic territories in Switzerland and eastern France. The king of the Aedui, Diviciacus, went to Rome requesting aid against the Germans, reminding them of old alliances and promising that his tribe would be loyal to the Roman interest.

Celtic power continued to contract elsewhere also. In the far east, the Galatian settlements of Asia Minor survived, but only through a strategic dependence on Roman power. Less further east, disaster loomed when the Dacian king Boerebistas united the Daci, Getae and Boeri into one kingdom. In the year 60 BC Boerebistas attacked the Celtic tribes of the area, the Scordisci, Boii, and Taurisci. He had a huge army—reported to have numbered 200,000 men—and he gained his most notable success near to the river Tisza in Hungary, where he routed the forces of the Boii king Critasiros. The Boii were pursued as far as the west bank of the Danube, and the Celtic tribes in general were soon pushed back through Bohemia and into their original area north of the Alps. The Celts in their homeland were thus coming under pressure from three sides at once—from Germanic tribes in the north, from Dacians in the east, and from the Romans in the south. The latter threat, in the guise of Caesar, was to be the most devastating of all.

There was turmoil in the Transalpine region, where the Boii and others from the east had

ABOVE: Figure on a coin of the Aeduian leader Dumnorix (here written Dubnorex), who was assassinated on the orders of Julius Caesar. The figure may represent the great Gaulish patriot himself. Now in Cabinet des Médailles, Bibliothèque Nationale, Paris.

been thrown back upon the incumbent peoples, where the Helvetii had similarly been pushed from the north, and where the Arverni and Allobroges had been crushed by the Romans. It was into this vortex of contracted territory, tribal rivalry, and general frustration that Caesar entered. The Helvetii were situated between the river Rhine, the Jura mountains, and Lake Geneva, and they wished to migrate to an area which would be safer from German attacks. Their leading chieftain, Orgetorix, had for years been planning to make room by extirpating the Roman influence from Transalpine Gaul, and to this purpose he had cemented agreements with Casticus, son of the former king of the Sequani to the west, and with Dumnorix, a chieftain of the Aedui and brother of their pro-Roman king Diviciacus. Further tension in the area was averted by Orgetorix's death, but in 58 BC, the Helvetii en masse decided to migrate southwards through the Roman province of Gallia Narbonensis.

Caesar immediately began to muster a large army in the neighbourhood of Geneva, and had the bridge over the river Rhône destroyed. The Helvetii appealed to him to allow them to pass peacefully through the Roman province, but he delayed an answer as he built up his army. In reality, he had no intention of acceding to the request, and in his own War Commentary he makes it clear that he thirsted after revenge for the defeat inflicted by the Tigurini on the Romans at Agen almost 50 years before. He fortified the banks of the Rhône, and then forbade the Helvetii to cross. Some of them attempted to do so, nevertheless, but were driven back by the Roman soldiers. Now Dumnorix the Aeduian made representations to the Sequani to allow the Helvetii to pass through their territory. He was a generous and popular man, and he secured an agreement between these two tribes and an exchange of hostages to underline it.

Although the intended passage did not touch on the Roman province, Caesar chose to regard it as threatening, and he raised two new legions in Italy and rushed to the area. He attacked the final group of the Helvetii, the Tigurini, as they crossed the river Saône, and slaughtered many of them. Immediately, the elderly Helvetian king, Divico, went in person to him to offer peace. He said that they were willing to settle only in a region which would please Caesar, but warned that if they were forced into war they might well destroy his army for 'they had learned from their fathers and ancestors to fight like brave men and not to rely on trickery or stratagem'. Taking this as a hint at the defeat which Divico himself had long ago inflicted on the Romans, Caesar answered haughtily and demanded hostages. Divico replied that the Helvetii were accustomed to accept hostages, but not to give them, and then he departed.

The Helvetii raised their camp and set off on their journey, and Caesar followed them closely for two weeks with his cavalry and legions. Finally, at Bibracte (a hill-fort on Mont Beuvray, west of Autun), the two armies came to grips. The Helvetii formed a phalanx, but in the fighting their spears were so long that they began to hinder each other. They began to retreat towards a hill, and the pursuing Romans were suddenly attacked on their right flank by thousands of Boii and Tulingi. The fighting lasted from midday until night, and finally the Celts left the field. Caesar had captured a son and daughter of Orgetorix, but about 130,000 Celtic warriors had survived the battle. These marched for three days through the territory of the Lingones and, finally, reduced by hunger and harassed by the Romans and their allies, they surrendered. Six thousand men of the Verbigeni tribe slipped away, hoping to escape to Germanic territory, but Caesar issued threats against anybody who helped them, and as a result they were

Julius Caesar (100-44 BC), ruthless opponent and conqueror of the Gauls. Statue now in British Museum, London.

brought back. Caesar executed them all, but allowed the Helvetii and their other allies to return home. He directed the Allobroges to supply them with food until their crops grew again, and persuaded the Aedui to accept the Boii on their territory. This leniency was dictated by Caesar's concern to maintain the Celts as a bulwark against German expansion.

His foresight proved correct, for Diviciacus soon pointed out to him that all the Gaulish tribes of the area wished to throw off the yoke of the Germanic overlord, Ariovistus, who was treating them with great cruelty. Fearing that the power of Ariovistus would continue to grow and that he would in time threaten Italy, Caesar decided to act against him and sent envoys demanding a meeting with him. After some delay, this meeting was held in the area of Alsace, where their respective armies had drawn close to each other near Vesontio (modern Besançon). Ariovistus spoke as an equal to Caesar, reminding him that both of them were there as conquerors and suggesting that they carve up Gaul between them. Caesar was peeved at this frankness, and demanded that Ariovistus withdraw all his forces back across the Rhine. Soon after, the two armies clashed and the result was a complete victory for the Romans, most of the Germans being killed and Ariovistus himself barely escaping with his life.

Belgae Peoples Prepare For War Against Romans

Caesar then left his army in winter quarters in that area, which was the territory of the Sequani, and he himself returned to Italy. Repeated reports began to reach him, however, that the tribes of north-eastern Gaul – who knew that they would soon be invaded by the Romans – were preparing for war. These were the Belgae, a very numerous Celtic people with roots around the Moselle and Rhine, but who had been spreading for many centuries into the rest of Gaul. They had developed into a loose confederation of tribes, including the Bellovaci, Suessiones, Treveri, Nervii, Atrebates, Eburones, and Remi. Several groups of them had also crossed the sea and settled in the south-east of Britain, and these maintained links with their Continental cousins. These numerous and widespread Belgae peoples had been ruled within living memory by a very powerful king of the Suessiones called Diviciacus, and in his War Commentary Caesar states that their king in his time was called Galba, 'a just and able man'.

Caesar raised two further legions in Italy, and rushed back to Gaul in the spring of 57 BC. The Remi, who were the southernmost of the Belgae, immediately sent their leading men, Iccius and Andecombogius, to him, offering an alliance and hostages; but the rest of the Belgae held firm. Caesar now sent Diviciacus of the Aedui to raid the lands of the Bellovaci, but the Belgae had already concentrated their forces and advanced to besiege Bibrax (modern Bievre), a town of the Remi. Here they used what Caesar described as the typical Gaulish method of laying siege, 'surrounding the whole circuit of the wall with a large number of men and showering stones at it from all sides', and then locking their shields over their heads, advancing close up, and undermining the wall.

Bibrax was showered in this way with stones and javelins, and the commander of the town, Iccius, could not have held out for long if Caesar had not rushed some forces to relieve him. The Belgae then set out in force to attack Caesar's own camp. Caesar was cautious, knowing that the Belgae had a great reputation for courage, and he had trenches on each side of his camp, with redoubts and artillery. Having used his cavalry to test the enemy, he drew up his lines for battle. After a brief skirmish, he decided on one of his favourite tactics, a feint, leading his infantry back into his camp and causing the Belgae to rush triumphantly after them. Caesar counter-attacked as the pursuers waded through the river Aisne, and after a fierce struggle the Belgae withdrew. The Bellovaci were anxious to return to their own territory, which was being ravaged by the Aedui, and the general Belgic force broke up for the moment to await what the Romans would do next. Caesar sent out his legions to attack them next morning as they dispersed, and all day long the pursuing Romans wrought havoc on the Belgae warriors.

He now decided to reduce the tribes of the Belgae one by one, and this he did by taking their hill-forts. The method he usually employed was to pile up earth against these strongholds and to erect towers and catapults for the assault. The Suessiones soon surrendered at their principal hill-fort, and he took hostages from them, including the sons of King Galba. Next he besieged the Bellovaci stronghold, and accepted their surrender after the intercession of Diviciacus on their behalf. The Ambiani also surrendered to him, but their neighbours the Nervii vowed not to submit to the Romans. The Nervii had a strong martial tradition, and they persuaded the Atrebates and the Viromandui to join with them in their resistance. Also, some of the surrendered Belgae were giving secret information to the Nervii on the deployment of

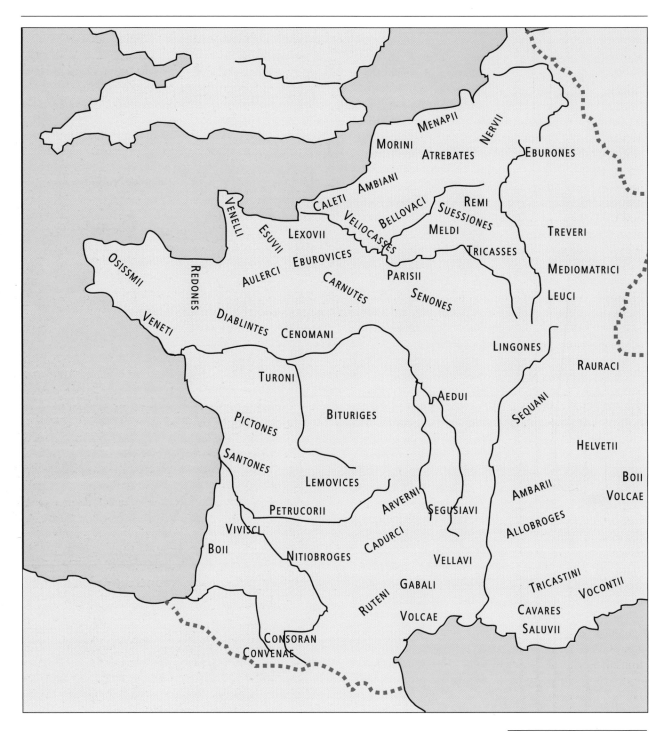

The areas inhabited by major Gaulish tribes in the 1st Century BC.

the Romans, especially the fact that each legion marched on its own and at a far distance from the others. Caesar says that the Nervii had no cavalry, and that they specialised in arranging obstacles such as cut saplings, hedges, and briars for the horsemen of their foes.

When he got word of the information seeping through to the Nervii, Caesar astutely had his legions march close together. Nevertheless, when they encamped near the Sambre, a wide river with steep banks, they were suddenly attacked by the Nervii, who charged on foot across the river with incredible speed. The Romans were taken by surprise, and their Numidian cavalry fled, but the legions held their ground against waves of Nervii. Caesar's lieutenant Labienus, who had been at the rear with two legions accompanying the baggage, now joined the fray, and the Romans rallied. The tide of battle turned, but the Nervii and their allies disdained to flee. Even in their desperate plight, Caesar says, they 'showed such bravery that, when their front ranks had fallen, those immediately behind stood on their prostrate bodies to fight; and when these too fell and the corpses were piled high, the survivors kept hurling javelins as though from the top of a mound, and flung back the spears intercepted by their shields'. Fighting to a finish, almost the whole nation of Nervii warriors were annihilated in that battle.

Meanwhile, a legion which Caesar had sent to the Atlantic seaboard in the north-west under Publius Crassus, son of the famous Crassus, had succeeded in subjecting Celtic tribes of that region. These included the Veneti, Venelli, Osissmi, Alerci and others and, as usual, hostages were taken from them. Taking care to quarter his legions for the following winter in the territories he had recently conquered and in central Gaul, Caesar then returned to Italy and Illyria, where he wished to inspect how the Roman method of governing other peoples was progressing. While he was there, a legion which he had left under Servius Galba to establish a permanent safe passage through the Alps was attacked and badly mauled by the Celtic mountain tribesmen of the area—the Nantuates, Veragri, and Seduni. Although the Romans succeeded in routing their attackers, killing about 10,000 of them, they had little choice but to abandon their efforts and withdraw to the safety of Provence.

CAESAR SCORES NAVAL VICTORY OFF BRITTANY

In the north-east of Gaul, the Veneti, Venelli and other peoples were smarting under the rule of Publius Crassus, and eventually they rebelled and took some Roman officers hostage, demanding the release of their own hostages in return. Caesar ordered ships to be built on the Loire, and he rejoined his troops in Gaul again in the spring of 56 BC. As his army advanced towards the north-east by land, he had his new naval squadron sail up the Loire to the Atlantic and there skirt the coast towards the territory of the Veneti in Brittany. After some initial difficulties, his navy defeated the Veneti at sea in full view of his land-troops. Then Caesar reduced the hill-forts of the Veneti and their allies, and after their surrender he treated them mercilessly — executing their leaders and selling all their population into slavery. Caesar's lieutenant Sabinus was equally successful in his campaign against the Venelli. Sabinus used a Gaulish double-agent to instil false confidence into the Venelli, who forced their leader Viridovix to attack the Roman camp against his better judgement. The result was a disaster, a large number of the Venelli being slaughtered and most of the rest captured.

Caesar next sent Publius Crassus to reduce the Celtic and Iberian inhabitants of the south-west. There the Romans met with stiff opposition from the Sotiates under their leader Adiatuanus, until the chief town of that tribe was taken. The Sotiates surrendered, and then Crassus set out to attack other tribes of the area, the Vocates and Tarusates. These people called on all their neighbours to support them, and even brought veterans of Sertorius's campaign in Spain to their assistance. After a fierce onslaught on their camp, the combined Celtic and Iberian forces were routed, and many more tribes of the area then surrendered. Towards the end of the summer, Caesar himself led an attack on the Morini and Menapii, tribes of the Belgae on the shore of the North Sea who had not yet surrendered. The Morini and Menapii withdrew into the forests, creating difficulties for Caesar, and the onset of bad weather forced him to withdraw.

Model of Celtic warrior with weapons, armour and dress as would have been common in northern Gaul and Britain in the 1st Century BC.

Virtually the whole of Gaul was now in Caesar's hands, and in 55 BC he defeated large forces of the Usipetes and Tenctheri, Germanic tribes who had been pushed by the Suebi into the north-east of Gaul. He then crossed the Rhine on a short campaign, slaughtering the people and laying waste the land in Germanic areas so as to deter any future incursions. Finally, as that summer drew to a close, he determined on an even more adventurous course, to cross the sea into Britain. He claimed that the reason for doing this was to gain vengeance for assistance given by the Belgic tribes in the south of Britain to their Continental cousins, but the real reason for his action is likely to have been to gain glory in Rome for conquests as far as the borders of the known world.

He sent a chieftain of the Atrebates, called Commius, across to Britain ahead of him, to secure the submission of the Britons, but the latter seized Commius and held him as a captive. Leaving some of his forces to guard the ports, Caesar crossed with two legions from the territory of the Morini, using about 80 transport boats and a number of warships. Arriving on the British coast, he found cavalry and chariots waiting to attack him. His men had difficulty in landing, but once on shore at Walmer, just north of Dover, they routed the enemy, who soon sent envoys with Commius offering to surrender. Caesar took hostages from them, and they promised to bring more hostages from the interior.

The transport ships bringing Caesar's cavalry ran into foul weather, however, and had to return to the Continent. Furthermore, many of his beached ships were damaged by the storm and, on learning this, the chiefs of the Britons decided to renew hostilities. In the ensuing battle, the Britons showed their style of fighting, by driving their chariots all around the Romans while hurling javelins, and then retiring and fighting on foot. Caesar noticed their great ability at controlling the chariot-horses: 'They can run along the chariot pole, stand on the yoke, and get back into the chariot as quick as lightning.' He very wisely withdrew his soldiers to their camp and, after several days of bad weather, he engaged the foe again and put them to flight. He now demanded twice as many hostages as before, saying that these should be sent after him to the Continent, and then he embarked and returned to Gaul before the weather got even worse. There he found the Morini again engaged in rebellion, and after a punitive

ABOVE: Cavalry of Julius Caesar crossing the Thames. The British Celts under Cassivellaunus tried to prevent the crossing by thrusting stakes and a stockade into the river. (From a fanciful painting by Charles D Ward.)

RIGHT: Modern representation of the Eburones leader Ambiorix, who organised a strong rebellion against the forces of Caesar. Ambiorix eluded all efforts to capture him, and finally escaped to safety beyond the Rhine. Statue in bronze at Tongres, Belgium, by Jules Bertin.

expedition against them he quartered his legions on Belgic territory for the winter, before himself returning again to Italy.

Hostages arrived from only two of the British tribes, however, and so Caesar determined on a second invasion of Britain. In the spring of 54 BC. But he found that he must first of all deal with the Treveri, who had refused to submit to him. Two rivals were contending for the leadership of that tribe – Indutiomarus and Cingetorix—and Caesar astutely used this division for his purpose. He first accepted the surrender of Cingetorix, and as a result Indutiomarus found excuses to make peace also. Caesar took hostages from both, and then hurried on with his preparations for a crossing to Britain. He had an established practice of keeping hostages from all the major Gaulish tribes with him so as to discourage rebellion, and he now paid particular attention to the Aedui leader Dumnorix. Caesar had distrusted Dumnorix from the beginning, describing him as 'a man of boundless courage, extremely popular with the masses because of his liberality, and an ardent revolutionary'.

He would, indeed, have killed Dumnorix long before but for the risk of alienating his old ally Diviciacus, who was Dumnorix's older brother. Now he demanded that Dumnorix accompany him to Britain, and the latter used several excuses —claiming that he was afraid of the sea and also that he was forbidden to leave Gaul because of religious considerations. When Caesar did not relent, Dumnorix slipped out of the camp with some horsemen, and Caesar sent a detachment of cavalry after him with orders to bring him back dead or alive. When he was surrounded, Dumnorix fought fiercely with sword in hand, and was cut down as he continued to shout out that 'he was a free man and a citizen of a free state'.

Following this, Caesar set sail for Britain with five legions and 2,000 cavalry in 600 boats. This time he had a carefree landing, but as soon as camp was set up he was attacked by cavalry and war-chariots. He put these to flight, but as he advanced inland he was repeatedly attacked by the Britons, who came swooping out of the woods when least expected. The commander of the united British tribes was Cassivellaunus, king of the Belgic Catuvellauni, who had been for some time attempting to enforce his authority on other tribes in the south of the island. Eventually, Cassivellaunus decided against engaging Caesar in pitched battles and kept his distance from the Roman legions as they advanced across the Thames and into his territory.

Caesar now used his old trick of divide and conquer, by restoring a young prince called Mandubracios to his tribe. This young man was the son of the Trinovantes king who had been killed by Cassivellaunus, and had gone to the Continent to seek Caesar's protection. The ploy of rekindling old animosities between the Britons proved successful, and soon several tribes came over to Caesar's side. Advancing to the main hill-fort of Cassivellaunus, he attacked it and forced the defenders to abandon it. It was, Caesar wrote, a typical British Celtic stronghold, in a densely wooded location and fortified with a rampart and trench.

Cassivellaunus, undeterred, called on several kings from the region of Kent to join his efforts, and they attacked the Roman naval camp on the coast there. The attack failed, and Cassivellaunus finally sent envoys to Caesar, offering peace and using Commius as an intermediary. Caesar, who was anxious to return to the Continent before winter set in, accepted the offers, on condition that Mandubracios and his Trinovantes not be molested, that a tribute be paid annually to the Roman government, and that hostages be handed over. Cassivellaunus was glad to accept these conditions, knowing that the Romans would soon be out of the way, and Caesar then returned to the Continent, leaving no permanent power-structure to subdue the Britons.

The Gauls were soon in rebellion again. This time it was the Eburones, who lived between the Meuse and the Rhine and were led by Ambiorix and Catuvolcus. The Eburones were encouraged by the Treveri chief Indutiomarus, whom Caesar had good reason already to distrust. Ambiorix, a skilled leader, threatened a Roman legion under Sabinus and Cotta who were encamped in his territory at Atuatuca. The Romans claimed that Ambiorix misled the legionaries by protestations of friendship, before attacking them and slaughtering them almost to a man. At any rate, 6,000 Romans fell during the battle, the greatest single defeat which Caesar's forces suffered in all of his campaigns in Gaul.

Ambiorix then set about enlisting many Gaulish tribes in his rebellion, including the Nervii. In an all-out attack on the camp of Quintus Tullius Cicero, brother of the orator, they employed Roman techniques which they had learned from captives. These included throwing up earthworks, constructing towers, and using ballistics. After several days of fighting, a messenger got through the Gaulish lines and summoned the help of Caesar, who quickly assembled legions from different parts of Gaul and marched to relieve the siege. On his approach, the whole Gaulish force of about 60,000 men went to meet him, but they were routed.

Ambiorix Elusive in Revolt Against Romans

All through the winter there were disturbances, and all the Gaulish tribes—with the exceptions of the Aedui and Remi—were inclined towards revolt. Indutiomarus hosted a great assembly, at which he announced his intention to banish the Romans. He was joined by the Eburones, Carnutes and Senones—whose council had dethroned Caesar's nominee Cavarinus from their kingship. In a surprise attack, however, the cavalry of Labienus succeeded in slaying Indutiomarus, bringing his head back to their camp in triumph.

Caesar was so alarmed at developments that he sent for three fresh legions from Pompey in Italy. Then he ravaged the territories of the Nervii and Senones, forcing their surrender and that of the Carnutes. He next marched north against the Menapii, forcing them to submit to him for the first time. Meanwhile, Labienus, by pretending to retreat, tricked the Treveri into attacking his force before German support arrived. The Treveri were defeated, and Caesar's ally Cingetorix was restored to the kingship. Caesar then again crossed the Rhine, to ensure that promised German support for Ambiorix did not materialise. The Suebi—who had been involved in negotiations with the Gauls—withdrew to the east of their territory, and Caesar decided not to follow but returned through the Ardennes to fight the Eburones, sending a cavalry detachment ahead to try to capture Ambiorix. The house of Ambiorix was in a wood, and the Romans came suddenly upon him. He barely escaped with his life, being placed on horseback and sent away by his loyal followers as they engaged the Romans.

Seeing no remaining chance of success, Ambiorix advised his allies to disperse, and he himself retreated to the forests with a small band of horsemen. His fellow-leader of the Eburones, Catuvolcus, committed suicide by poisoning himself with the juice of a yew-tree. Caesar advanced through the territory of the Eburones, slaughtering the inhabitants and spreading famine everywhere, and several times his forces came near to capturing Ambiorix. The determined Eburones leader, he wrote, 'would escape by hiding in a wood or ravine, and under cover of night would make off in some new direction—escorted only by four horsemen, for to no one else did he dare entrust his life.' Caesar finally gave up the pursuit, and called a council at the Remi town of Durocortorum (modern Reims), where he reasserted his authority over the Gauls and had the Senones patriot Acco, who had inspired the revolt, put to death by flogging and beheading.

In his War Commentary, Caesar would have the reader believe that his purpose was to bring stability to Gaul, but he fails to explain why the Gauls repeatedly rebelled against his rule and were even willing to invite German aid, and why his Aeduian and Remi allies continued to intercede with him on behalf of defeated rebels. The general situation is nowhere more clear

Plan of the grave of a Celtic leader, buried in a tumulus with his chariot and other possessions in the 5th Century BC at Somme-Brienne, in the Département of Marne, France. Such tumuli were centres of veneration for the Gauls.

than in the case of the greatest revolt of all, which began at the start of 53 BC. The Gauls were livid at the treatment meted out to Acco, and resigned themselves 'to die in battle' rather than suffer 'the loss of their ancient military glory and the liberty inherited from their ancestors'. The Carnutes, under their leader Gutuator, called on all tribes to unite in the common cause, and 'to stack their military standards together' as was their symbolic custom. They then attacked the Roman settlers in Cenabum (modern Orléans) and slew them, and word passed quickly throughout Gaul that the rising had begun.

The leadership was given to a young prince of the Arverni, the powerful tribe who inhabited the area west of the Cevennes mountains. He was called Vercingetorix, and his father Celtillus had been the most powerful man in all Gaul but had been killed in internecine fighting. Vercingetorix had independently recruited young men of different areas to his cause, and now that many tribes supported him he prepared for a final conflict with Rome. He was a great speaker, who could easily win the customary approval of Gaulish warriors by cheering and clashing their weapons together. But he was also a shrewd campaigner, not prone to impetuosity like so many Celtic leaders, and proved himself a match for Caesar in strategy. Caesar himself rushed to the territory of the Helvetii, and from there began to harass the Arverni in the hope of luring Vercingetorix into open battle. Vercingetorix, however, chose instead to attack the Boii, who were at that time in alliance with Rome.

Caesar realised that Vercingetorix was trying to extend the Roman lines, but had no choice but to go to the defence of his allies. On his way, he captured the Senones stronghold of Vellaunodunum, but as soon as he reached the territory of the Bituriges he found his army

Gaulish coins showing Vercingetorix at various stages of his life. The most celebrated of all Celtic leaders, he proved a match for Juius Caesar in military strategy until his defeat at the hill-fort of Alesia in Burgundy. He was ignominiously put to death in Rome in 46 BC. Coins in Cabinet des Médailles, Bibliothèque Nationale, Paris.

being shadowed by that of Vercingetorix. After a few minor engagements, Vercingetorix decided on a scorched earth policy, hoping to weaken the Romans by a combination of harassment and starvation. All of the Gaulish towns in the path of the Romans were destroyed, with the exception of Avaricum (modern Yèvre), which the Bituriges prevailed on Vercingetorix to spare against his better judgement. When Caesar besieged that town, Vercingetorix encamped near to him on a hill. The Gauls, using tactics learned from the Romans, attacked Caesar's camp with rocks and torches flung from towers and platforms, but the attack failed and the Romans took the town and massacred all its inhabitants.

Vercingetorix wisely decided to bide his time and, as Caesar's legions set out on the march towards the great Arverni hill-fort of Gergovia (modern La Roche Blanche), he brought his army along on the opposite side of the river Allier, making sure that all the bridges were broken to prevent the Romans from crossing. Caesar hid two of his legions in a forest, however, and when Vercingetorix had passed on he managed to rebuild a bridge and brought his own forces across. As a result he was able to besiege Gergovia. After a failed assault, in which he lost 700 men, Caesar offered battle to Vercingetorix's army, but after a few cavalry skirmishes the Gauls again backed away.

Vercingetorix's repeated calls to the Gaulish tribes to unite as one great force for liberty were, however, bearing fruit, even to the extent of splitting the Aedui, and Caesar now had to depart to the territory of that tribe to restore order there. The Aeduian rebels seized the town of Noviodunum (modern Nevers) and massacred the Roman garrison there. Caesar became anxious for the welfare of his legions which were with Labienus in that area laying waste the territory of the Senones. His anxiety was well founded, for the Bellovaci, reputedly the best fighters in Gaul, had joined the rebellion.

With all Gaul in turmoil, Vercingetorix held a great council at Bibracte, which was attended by almost all the leading tribes. There he was confirmed in command, and he explained his policy of avoiding a pitched battle and wearing down the Romans by destroying all the provisions of the countryside. 'Destroy your corn and burn your granaries,' he told them, 'and this sacrifice will make you free men forever!'

Caesar recruited Germanic mercenaries and set out to defend the borders of Gallia Narbonensis in the south, giving the impression that he was in full retreat. Vercingetorix followed him, and could not refrain from attacking the Romans on the march. However, the combined Roman and German cavalry proved more than equal to their Gaulish counterparts in these attacks, and Vercingetorix was compelled to withdraw to the hill-fort of Alesia to regroup. Caesar pursued him there and encamped near to the stronghold. The tide had turned, and Vercingetorix felt it necessary to send his horsemen in all directions to muster more recruits. Soon his force of 80,000 warriors was being besieged by Caesar's legions, who began to construct elaborate siege-works all around. The Gaulish tribes convened a great council in the territory of the Aedui, and all agreed to send a relief force to rescue Vercingetorix's army, and even Caesar's old ally Commius joined in the effort. The result was—according to Caesar—that a force of 8,000 horse and 250,000 infantry set out to the relief. These numbers must be exaggerated, but the force was no doubt a considerable one.

Gaulish Forces Struggle Against Romans And German Mercenaries

When the army of Vercingetorix, cut off by the Roman encirclement and reduced to cannibalism for want of food, caught sight of the relief force approaching, they were overwhelmed with joy, and sent out a large cavalry detachment, interspersed with archers and infantry, to give battle to the Romans. Caesar immediately ordered his own cavalry into action. All day long the battle raged, in full view of the main Roman army and the two Gaulish armies, but in the end Caesar's German mercenaries broke the Gaulish lines.

Two days later, the whole Gaulish relief force attacked the Roman camp, and Vercingetorix led his forces out of the stronghold to join the fighting. The Gauls were encumbered by all the fortifications which Caesar had erected, however, and they were again repulsed. Next day the Gauls made another mighty effort to break through the Roman fortifications, but Caesar ordered a counter-attack and in ferocious hand-to-hand fighting the Gaulish forces finally broke and retired from the field.

The relief army dispersed soon afterwards, and Vercingetorix was again cut off within the stronghold. He spoke to his men, reminding them that he had not undertaken the war for his own benefit but for the freedom of his people. He was now willing, he said, to give himself up in order to assuage the Roman anger, and so he put on his most beautiful armour, had his horse carefully groomed, and rode out through the gates of Alesia. Approaching the seated Caesar, he rode around him on his horse, before leaping from it, stripping off his armour, and throwing himself on the ground. Vercingetorix was taken in chains to Rome, where he was imprisoned in a filthy cellar.

After the surrender, Caesar gave the vast bulk of the Gaulish army as slaves to his own soldiers, and in the following winter he embarked on a punitive campaign against the Carnutes, who had started the revolt. Their leader Gutuator joined in a futile resistance with the Bituriges and Bellovaci. Commios led the combined force, but eventually had to flee to safety across the Rhine. Gutuator was captured by Caesar and, like Acco before him, was flogged savagely and then beheaded. Sporadic resistance continued, but no hope remained, and in 46 BC Vercingetorix was beheaded in Rome as part of Caesar's triumphant celebrations.

On his return home, Caesar soon clashed with his equally ambitious colleague Pompey. In the ensuing civil war—fought out on the broad stage of the growing Roman empire—Pompey was murdered and Caesar assumed complete mastery. His lust for power had been satiated, but at the cost of millions of Celtic and other lives. However, he was not to enjoy his power for long,

Stylised silver coin of the Diablintes tribe showing warrior in chariot. Such abstract depictions were common in Gaulish numismatics, and may have referred to ritual or mythical themes.

for in 44 BC he was stabbed to death by a mixed cabal of friends and foes. Before his death, Caesar had the experience of meeting one Celtic leader who was comparable to himself in deviousness. This was Deïotarus, a chieftain in Asia Minor, who had survived a mass-slaughter of Galatian nobles by the king of Pontus, Mithridates V, in 88 BC. Deïotarus had taken the Roman side in the war against Mithridates, and was made king of Galatia by Pompey, as a result of which he had fought on the side of his benefactor in the Roman civil war.

When the victorious Caesar arrived in Asia Minor in 47 BC, Deïotarus met him in the dress of a suppliant, and was ordered by the great conqueror to resume his royal attire. The rivals of Deïotarus wished to dethrone him, however, and his own grandson accused him of an attempt on the life of his all-powerfull guest. The case was heard by Caesar himself in Rome, with the orator Cicero defending Deïotarus. The verdict was put on hold, and the assassination of Caesar may have saved the old rogue. He was soon restored to all his territory in Galatia by Marcus Antonius. He changed sides again, supporting Caesar's assassins for a while, before returning once more to his loyalty to Antonius and living out a long life. One may speculate on how such a Machiavellian character might have handled affairs if he had been in authority at the other end of the Celtic world.

Chapter 7

SURVIVAL IN THE WEST

After the death of Deïtarus, his son Deitarus II became king of Galatia, but he made a fatal mistake by supporting his father's patron Marcus Antonius against Octavian, who became the first Roman Emperor with the title of Augustus. Upon the triumph of Augustus, Galatia became a province of the Roman Empire, thus ending forever Celtic power in the east. By this time, the power of the Celts had been completely broken in the whole land-mass of Europe and in the Middle East. Their only importance was in the realm of military service, and it is interesting to note that the famous Graeco-Egyptian queen Cleopatra had Galatian Celts in her army. She gave 400 of these to the Jewish king Herod Philip, and this troop figured prominently in the funeral service for Herod the Great in the year 4 BC.

Neither was there any Celtic revival on the Danube, for after the death of the Thracian king Boerabistas the Romans moved into his territory and in the year 8 AD Augustus made that whole area also into a Roman province. In Gaul a whole new socio-economic structure was being built, the purpose of which was to completely Romanise the area. This followed the pattern which had earlier been applied to Iberia—i.e., the construction of a network of new roads so as to facilitate the military dominance and commercial system of the Empire, and the recruiting of the warrior class of the Celts into the Roman army. The latter aspect of the conquest was crucial, for it guaranteed the re-education of the Celts into Roman ways and correspondingly weakened all aspects of their culture and identity.

It is notable that after this period Gaulish leaders are referred to by Roman names, although they doubtless had their own native names also. Romanisation, however, did not bring contentment. The imperialist exploitation was soon felt, particularly in the

RIGHT: A bronze shield of the 1st Century AD found in the River Thames at Battersea. The elaborate bronze sheeting and decoration with red enamel show that it was used for ceremonial purposes rather than for fighting. It may have been placed in the river as a votive deposit. Now in British Museum, London.

LEFT: Celtic bronze helmet, found near Waterloo Bridge in the River Thames, England. It measures 16.5in (42cm) between the horns, and dates from the early 1st Century AD. It may once have decorated a shrine by the riverside. Now in British Museum, London.

case of overwhelming taxes, and this was the cause of a rebellion which broke out in 21 AD. The leaders were Julius Florus of the Treveri and Julius Sacrovir of the Aedui, an unusual alliance in view of previous history. Both were trained military men of the Roman army, and as well as appealing to their tribes they also sought support from serving Roman soldiers.

First to take the field were the Turoni and Andecavi in the Alpine region, and Florus felt constrained with other Gauls to give support in their suppression. He put on a display of helping the Romans in the fighting, but kept his head uncovered, which caused suspicion that he wished to be recognised by the rebels and so spared. He then prevailed on some of the Treveri cavalry to join him in revolt, but was defeated by some of his own tribesmen sent by the Romans to oppose him. He successfully eluded pursuit for some time, and when no hope was left he took his own life.

The Aeduian Sacrovir was more successful, seizing the tribal capital of Bibracte, which had been renamed Augustodunum (modern Autun). He first got the support of the tribal youth, arming them with whatever weapons he had managed to accumulate, and then recruited slaves who were being trained by the Romans as gladiators. Soon his force amounted to 40,000, and he won the support of the Sequani, who were in turn ravaged by two Roman legions. When the Romans approached Bibracte, they found the forces of Sacrovir drawn up on a plain to confront them, with Sacrovir himself on a splendid horse in the frontline. After fierce fighting, Sacrovir retreated to the fortress, and then with a few followers took refuge in a country house. They were surrounded, and the house set on fire, but Sacrovir and his friends took their own lives in the flaming ruins rather than surrender.

Little of fighting spirit remained in Gaul. Only the islands in the west remained outside of the overbearing power of the Roman Empire, and this rankled. Caesar's invasions of Britain had been for prestige rather than for conquest, and he left no permanent force behind him. In fact, these invasions had the opposite effect, in that the man whom he had sent to negotiate, Commius of the Atrebates, later joined the rebellion against him in Gaul, and later still fled to the relative safety of Britain with many of his followers. There, in the area southwest of the Thames, Commius set up a kingdom in or about the year 51 BC. The Atrebates were Belgae, and as such were merely following the example of other groups of Belgae who had been settling in the south of Britain for generations.

It is not clear what attitude the strongest leader of these established groups, Cassivellaunus, took to Commius's arrival, but there is plenty of evidence of a rearrangement of power among the Celtic peoples of Britain in this period. Cassivellaunus was king of the Catuvellauni, who were situated in the wide area north of the Thames, their two strongest fortresses being Camulodunum (modern Colchester) and Verulamnium (on a plateau over the river Ver). Between the Catuvellauni and the sea in the east were the Trinovantes, whom Caesar had won into his alliance, but within a generation this tribe had come under the sway of one of Cassivellaunus' successors, called Cunobelinus.

The gradual extension of Cunobelinus's influence meant a displacing of other rulers. Some of these, well aware of the massive power across the sea, fled to Rome to seek assistance. Among such refugees was

Dubnovellaunus, displaced king of the Trinovantes, and Tincommius, son and successor of Commius as king of the Atrebates, both of whom appealed to Caesar Augustus around the year 6 BC. Others were to follow—including a son of Cunobelinus called Adminius, who fled to the Emperor Gaius, and another son of Commius, called Verica, who fled to the Emperor Claudius. Augustus had planned an invasion of Britain, and Gaius had boasted that Adminius had handed over Britain to him, but their plans were frustrated by affairs nearer home. Claudius was equally determined, and circumstances were more favourable to the project in his time. Another invasion was imminent when Cunobelinus died in or about the year 40 AD.

An invasion army of about 40,000 men set sail in 43 AD, under the command of Aulus Plautius. The leaders also included Flavius Sabinus and his younger brother, the future Emperor Vespasian. They disembarked in Kent, and found no major force ranged against them until they were crossing a river—probably the Medway. Here they were opposed by the sons of Cunobelinus, Caratacus and Togodumnus. During the first day's fighting, Plautius sent some of his soldiers to swim across the water and attack the Britons' chariots, and Vespasian soon led another company across the river at a different point. On the second day, a fresh attack was made by the main Roman body, and the Britons —under pressure from both sides of the water—fell back towards the mouth of the Thames. Here the same process was followed, and again the Britons were caught between Roman forces on both sides of the water. They suffered heavy losses, and soon after Togodumnus was killed in a skirmish.

The Romans waited for some time for the Emperor Claudius himself to land with fresh troops and an elephant corps, and then advanced swiftly on Camulodunum. The great citadel of the Catuvellauni was taken without much difficulty, for Caratacus had decided to vacate the area and to carry on the resistance further west. Claudius then returned to the Continent, leaving Plautius to complete the conquest. Several of the tribes surrendered to the Romans, the first being the Dobunni of the Severn basin, and soon after the Atrebates, Trinovantes, and the powerful Iceni to the north of them. All of these were Belgae, but even the long established tribes of the interior soon began to waver. A major factor was the surrender of the Brigantes, who were ruled by Queen Cartismandua and dominated the whole area of northern England. The Romans quickly garrisoned the conquered territories, and within a few years were in complete control of all the eastern region from the Ouse to the Isle of Wight.

In 47 AD the command was handed over to Publius Ostorius Scapula. He followed a policy of coercion, and in the following winter several of the tribes rebelled. They were led by the Iceni, who so far had managed to avoid confrontation with the Romans and whose military strength was therefore undiminished. Although the Roman historian Tacitus states that the rebels 'performed many noble feats' in the ensuing fighting, they were quickly suppressed, and Ostorius then ravaged the western areas, where Caratacus had built up a powerful base among tribes such as the Cangi, Silures, and Ordovoci. Being chosen as their war-chief, Caratacus told his supporters that the imminent battle would decide between their freedom or slavery, and he encouraged them greatly by claiming that Julius Caesar himself had been forced to vacate the island. They put up a stubborn fight in the region of Gloucester, holding the Romans back for a long time with missiles, but when the legionaries came to close quarters the Britons—who lacked breastplates and helmets—were no match for them.

In this battle, the family of Caratacus was captured. He himself escaped northwards to the territory of the Brigantes, but Queen Cartismandua soon handed him over to the Romans. He and his family were taken to Rome and paraded as captives there in 50 AD. Tacitus says that the other prisoners pleaded for mercy, but not Caratacus. Speaking before the Emperor, he said that he was a king descended from illustrious ancestors and should not be expected to accept slavery. Claudius was so impressed by his demeanour that he granted a pardon to him and his family. It was reported that he wandered about Rome after being set free and, on seeing the size and splendour of the city, exclaimed: 'How can you, who have so many and such fine possessions, covet our poor tents?'

Back in Britain, however, the fighting continued, fuelled by the oppression and rapacity of Ostorius and his officers. The Silures raided the Roman garrison in their territory, causing heavy casualties, and then wiped out some Roman cavalry squadrons.

After the death of Ostorius in 52 AD, Aulus Didius was appointed in his place, but before he arrived in Britain a whole Roman legion was defeated by the Silures. Didius managed to stabilise the situation, driving the Silures further west and increasing Roman defences in the Severn Valley.

In the following years he had to deal with an awkward situation, for a civil war broke out between the Brigantes queen, Cartismandua, and her husband Venutius who was 'pre-eminent in military skill'. Cartismandua had caused the brother and other relatives of Venutius to be arrested, and as a result many of his tribe supported Venutius in a push against her. The Romans intervened on the side of Cartismandua, and a legion was sent north to oppose Venutius. Didius was too preoccupied with the Silures in the south-west, and so—after inflicting some setbacks on Venutius—the Romans were content to make an agreement with him which restored Cartismandua to power.

The next Roman governor, Veranius Nepos, boasted that he would make the whole of Britain subject to the new Emperor Nero, but he died within a year and his design was carried forward by his successor, Suetonius Paulinus. This governor brought his forces through north Wales as far as the Irish Sea, causing many refugees to seek shelter on the island of Mona (Anglesey). In the year 61 AD, Suetonius decided to attack this island. He took his infantry over on flat-bottomed vessels, while the cavalry forded or swam across. The defenders resorted to magical postures to frighten and weaken the Romans, and the description given by Tacitus captures the savage drama of what was to follow:

This slaughter was hardly over, however, when news reached Suetonius of a major revolt on the east coast of Britain. There the king of the Iceni, Prasutagus, had died, leaving the Roman Emperor as his heir in the hope that this would protect his people. The opposite was

the result, for his kingdom was plundered by the Roman veterans who had been settled there, the nobles of the Iceni were stripped of their power, and the king's relatives were enslaved. Prasutagus's widow Boudicca was flogged, and his two daughters were raped. As the people were evicted from their farms, a temple was erected to the late Emperor Claudius, who had been proclaimed divine, and this temple was regarded as a symbol of the Roman tyranny.

The Iceni could take no more, and when Suetonius with his legions was in the west they resorted to rebellion, urging the Trinovantes and others to join them. In the delirious atmosphere, a statue dedicated by the Romans to victory at Camulodunum fell prostrate, and this was seen by the Britons as a portent of the overthrow of their oppressors. The Roman historian Dio Cassius gives a description of Boudicca:

In stature she was very tall, in appearance most terrifying, in the glance of her eye most fierce, and her voice was harsh. A great mass of very tawny hair fell to her hips, around her neck was a large gold necklace, and she wore a tunic of varying colours, over which a thick mantle was fastened with a brooch.

Grasping a spear, she spoke to her people, calling them to arms. Dio quotes her speech and—even though the actual words which he attributes to her must be speculative—the general drift runs true to character. She complained that the Romans were crushing her people with taxes, and that the Britons should never have allowed them to seize power in the island. The Romans should, she said, have been expelled as their famous Julius Caesar was, and she then made a series of comparisons between the Romans and the Britons.

She said the Romans were born into bondage and were extremely protective of themselves, wearing helmets and breastplates and hiding behind palisades and trenches. The Britons, on the other hand, were born free, were so courageous that they fought without preparation and protected only by their shields, and they had such agility and skill that they could conceal themselves in swamps and mountains. The Romans required good food and clothing, whereas the Britons could survive on wild plants and water; the Romans required boats to cross rivers, whereas the Britons swam across naked. In typical warrior fashion, she compared the Romans to 'hares and foxes trying to rule over hounds and wolves', and then proceeded to other satirical comments. The Emperor Nero, she said, was an effeminate fop who played the lyre and tried to beautify himself. The Roman leaders were accustomed to have intercourse with boys, boys moreover who were past their prime! They were slaves to a lyre-player, and he was a bad musician at that!

A huge horde of Celtic warriors attacked and took Camulodunum and Verulamnium, and then seized all the surrounding countryside, slaughtering about 70,000 Romans, military and civilians alike. Suetonius brought his troops by forced marches through the hostile population to London—which was a Roman trading centre—but, realising that he could not hold it, he withdrew to what he considered a more favourable position, probably at modern St Albans, north of London. This, closed in at the rear by a forest, was approached by a narrow defile which opened onto a plain, where the Britons had assembled. Suetonius had about 10,000 soldiers with him, and these were outnumbered several times by the Iceni and their allies.

ABOVE: Dramatic monument of Boudicca in her war-chariot, accompanied by her daughters, on Westminster Bridge in London. Cast in bronze, it is the work of the 19th Century sculptor Thomas Thornycroft.

One report claims that Boudicca had over 200,000 warriors, but that must be an exaggeration. With her daughters, she drove in her chariot around tribe after tribe, encouraging them and saying that she was there, not as a noble, 'but as one of the people, avenging my lost freedom, my scourged body, and the outraged chastity of my daughters'. She concluded by telling them that in this battle they must conquer or die. 'This is a woman's resolve — as for the men, they may live and be slaves!' For his part, Suetonius called on his soldiers 'to continue the work of bloodshed and destruction', for after victory 'everything will be in your power!'

The Romans advanced silently, while the Britons shouted and sang battle-songs. Then the two armies joined, and ferocious fighting continued until late in the day, when the Britons retreated, many of them being put to flight and many others slain. The Romans set to slaughtering men, women and children, and the battle ended in a complete rout. Only about 400 Romans fell, compared to almost 80,000 Britons. Boudicca took poison to end her life, and the Romans — soon reinforced from the Continent — brought fire and sword to the tribes who had rebelled and even to those who had wavered. Eventually, news of Suetonius's savagery reached Rome, and he was recalled and replaced by a more merciful governor.

VINDEX MOVEMENT BRINGS ABOUT DEMISE OF NERO

Things were relatively calm for some years, but the extravagance of Nero and the general rapacity of Roman officials led to further increased taxation in Britain and Gaul. In 68 AD, an Aquitanian Gaul, Gaius Julius Vindex, called on his people to revolt against Nero, who had 'despoiled the whole Roman world' and whose crimes and buffoonery surpassed all description. Vindex was descended from the kings of his people and, since Gaulish nobles were accepted as Imperial citizens, he was a Senator at Rome. Dio describes him as 'powerful in body and of shrewd intellect, skilled in warfare and full of daring'. He now called on the Gauls to 'help themselves and help the Romans, and to liberate the whole world'.

Vindex's objective was not to free Gaul from the Roman yoke, but to place the more amenable Roman general Servius Sulpicius Galba on the throne. He gained the tacit support of several Gaulish tribes, including the Aedui, but others such as the Treveri and Lingones were hostile to him. Nero sent an army against Vindex, under the command of Rufus Gallus; but, instead of fighting, Rufus held a conference with him at Vesontio (modern Besancon). They agreed to co-operate against Nero, but some of Rufus's soldiers who were unaware of the agreement attacked Vindex's army and slew a great number of them. Vindex was so dispirited by the fiasco that he took his own life, but the movement which he had started continued to grow, leading to the abdication and suicide of Nero.

Civil war soon developed between the new Emperor Galba and his army on the Rhine, headed by Aulus Vitellius. Galba was assassinated, and his successor Otho had to deal with the continuing revolt, which gained the support of the Roman legions in northern Gaul and Britain. Most of the Gauls wavered, and Roman armies on both sides dealt disdainfully with them. Particularly brutal was the treatment meted out by the rebels to the Helvetii, who withheld their support and as a result thousands of them were massacred or sold into slavery. The legions of the Danube proclaimed Vespasian emperor and, to foment trouble for Vitellius, he encouraged a revolt by the king of the Batavi (in present-day Holland), who was called Julius Civilis. After the defeat of Vitellius, however, Civilis continued his attempts to free the Germanic tribes from Rome and, seeing his successes, the Gauls were tempted to join him.

Rumours began to spread that the Roman armies were suffering setbacks everywhere, and the druids pointed to a recent fire at the Capitol in Rome as a portent of the end of the Empire. The commander of the Treveri cavalry — called Julius Classicus — was a natural leader, being descended from the kings of his tribe. His boast was that his family 'had given to Rome more enemies than allies'. His own Treveri were to the fore in the revolt, and they were soon joined by the Lingones, Nervii, Tungri, and others. The Sequani and the Mediomatrici, however, remained loyal to Rome. Classicus sent an assassin to dispatch the Roman commander at Novaesium in Belgae territory, and then he himself entered the Roman camp there and administered an oath to 'the Empire of All Gaul'. Soon after, the Lingones leader called Julius Sabinus led an attack on the Sequani, but he was defeated and the Gauls began to waver.

The Remi — old allies of Rome — were spreading the message throughout Gaul that peace was preferable to freedom, and to settle the matter a conference was held between

Areas inhabited by the major tribes in Britain at the time of the Claudian invasion.

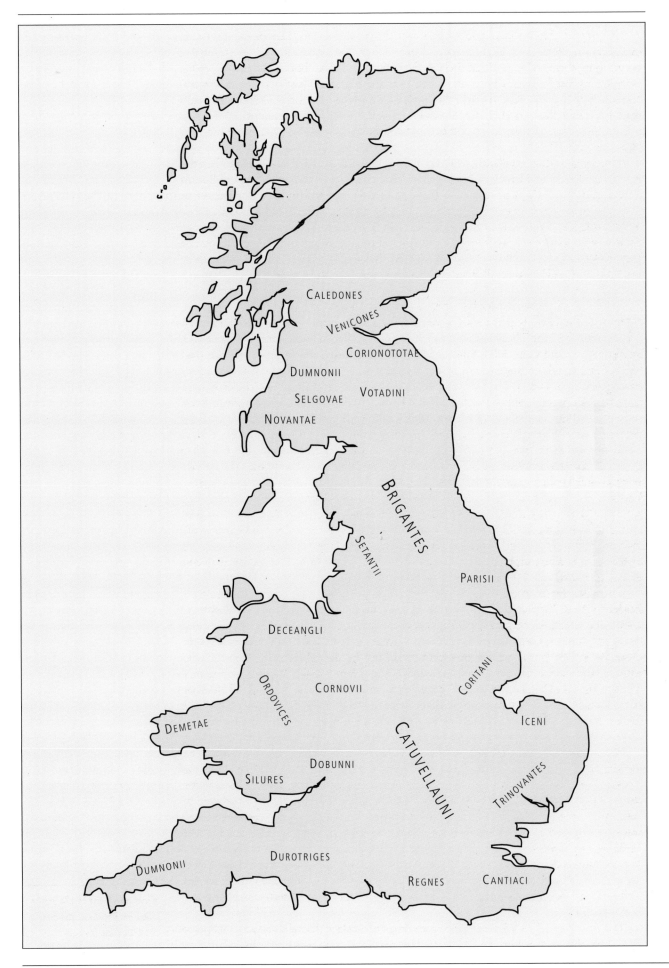

CALEDONES

VENICONES

CORIONOTOTAE

DUMNONII

SELGOVAE   VOTADINI

NOVANTAE

BRIGANTES

SETANTII

PARISII

DECEANGLI

CORITANI

ORDOVICES   CORNOVII

DEMETAE   ICENI

DOBUNNI   CATUVELLAUNI

SILURES   TRINOVANTES

DUMNONII   DUROTRIGES

REGNES   CANTIACI

various Gaulish tribes. A Treveri leader called Julius Valentinus made a fiery speech to the conference, but he was contradicted by Julius Auspex of the Remi, who warned that the Roman legions were approaching. The result of the conference—Tacitus tells us—was that 'while applauding Valentinus's courage, they followed the advice of Auspex'.

The Treveri and Lingones were left alone to continue the war. The Emperor Vespasian sent a huge army to the Rhineland under Petilius Cerialis, and he defeated them in several battles. Having taken Trier, the native town of Classicus, he had the Treveri and Lingones captives assembled before him and he addressed them, harping on the old Caesarian lie that the Romans were merely in Gaul to protect the Gauls from the Germans. Cerialis's army was soon besieged at Trier, however, by the combined forces of Classicus and Civilis. Civilis preferred to prolong the siege, but a Treveri leader called Julius Tutor argued for a quick attack, and Classicus agreed with this. They attacked by night, routing the Roman cavalry, and were putting the infantry to flight when Cerialis rallied them. The Gauls, thinking that victory was theirs, had begun to squabble over the spoils, when they were counter-attacked by the Romans and scattered. The two Treveri leaders, Classicus and Tutor, survived the debacle, and they were to the forefront with Civilis until their final defeat at Vetera (modern Xanten) in 70 AD.

In Britain, a year later, the Brigantes were again split between Venutius and his wife Cartismandua. Once again the Romans intervened, rescuing the queen, but Venutius survived and assumed complete leadership of his tribe. Now Vespasian sent Cerialis to Britain to suppress the Brigantes, and within three years Cerialis had achieved this, bringing that whole northern area under his control. His successor Frontinus subdued the Silures in south Wales and commenced a campaign against the Ordovoces in north Wales.

His successor in turn was the celebrated Cnaius Julius Agricola, who arrived in 78 AD. Agricola had served in Britain with both Suetonius and Cerialis, and was a hard-headed and ambitious soldier. He determined immediately to continue the campaign against the Ordovoces and, having defeated them he proceeded to Anglesey and retook it for the Romans without much effort. He reduced all of the south of Britain to the Pax Romana, and then placed a ring of garrisoned forts around each tribe and began to organise the social life of all the areas on the pattern of Imperial culture, making a special effort to educate the sons of chieftains in Roman manners.

In 81 AD Agricola led an army northwards, ravaging the country as far as the Tay estuary. Tacitus, his son-in-law, states that Agricola lined the side of

LEFT: Two stylised Gaulish coins showing warriors on horseback, apparently preparing to charge into battle.

RIGHT: Detail on a Pictish stone from the Manse, Galmis, on Tayside. As with Pictish language and inscriptions, the import of these figures has not yet been deciphered. They include a serpent, a fish, and what appears to be a hook.

Reconstruction of sling with some of a hoard of 11,000 balls found at Danebury excavation. They were used for hunting and fighting by the Celts. From the Museum of the Iron Age, Andover, Hampshire, England

Britain facing Ireland with fortresses, and that he used to say that Ireland itself could be taken and held by a single legion with a force of auxiliaries. An Irish prince, who had been expelled after a rebellion, came to Agricola, who kept him in the hope of using him in such an invasion. This project, however, never materialised, for Agricola considered it more urgent to subdue the Caledonian tribes in the north of Scotland. These tribes were a mixture of Celts and an earlier people whom the Romans called by the Latin name Picti ('painted ones'). The latter were an indigenous population, who spoke a pre-Indo-European language, but their power had been reduced by Celtic inroads into Britain since the 5th Century BC or thereabouts. By the time of the Roman invasion, their culture and language must have been heavily influenced by Celtic elements.

In the summer of 84 AD, Agricola gathered forces by land and sea for a strike even further northwards. Seeing the Roman fleet skirting the shore, the Caledonians realised that there was no escape left to them and therefore they determined to fight. They fell upon some of the new Roman fortresses and, as Agricola sent his army against them, they attacked the camp of his 9th legion by night. Agricola was warned of this by his scouts and went to relieve the camp, with the result that the Caledonians were caught between two Roman forces. They quickly retreated into the marshes and woods to reorganise and—Tacitus says—'to ratify their alliance with sacrificial rites'. Matters were drawing to a conclusion, and in the following summer Agricola took his army as far as 'Mons Graupius' (in the district of Moray Firth), where the Caledonians had established their headquarters. The tribes had assembled a large force there, and they were addressed by the foremost man among their leaders, 'a man of outstanding valour and nobility' called Calgacus. His name was a Celtic one, meaning 'swordsman'.

Tacitus quotes the speech which Calgacus was reported to have made, and it is an impressive one. He started by drawing attention to 'the united force which you are showing today', which would bring 'the dawn of freedom for all of Britain'. The Roman power had so expanded as to threaten even themselves, 'the most distant dwellers on earth, the last of the free'. Condemning the Romans as 'pillagers of the world', he said that 'they give the false name of government to robbery, butchery, and plunder—they create desolation and they call it peace'. Unless the Caledonians triumphed in battle, they would be robbed of their sustenance, crippled by building roads through forests and marches under the lash, their women would be defiled and all reduced to slavery. Previously, discord among the tribes had given the Romans the opportunity to control them, but now all would be inspired to regain their freedom. Beyond this army of Agricola there was nothing else to fear, for there were only forts without garrisons, colonies of aging veterans, and towns where the population was more than willing to rebel against tyranny.

This speech was greeted 'in barbarian fashion' by his followers with singing and shouting. The Caledonian forces were situated on higher ground, but their front line was on the plain and the others on the rising slopes behind them in series. In front of the whole force, facing the Romans on the plain, were the charioteers, making a great din. The Caledonians numbered about 30,000 men, and the Romans somewhat less. Agricola had his auxiliaries spread out in the front line, with his cavalry on the flanks, and the legionaries behind. The battle began with an exchange of missiles, with the Caledonians showing great skill at parrying the Roman javelins with their huge swords and small shields. Agricola then ordered a charge, and in the hand-to-hand fighting the Caledonians were at a disadvantage, for the short swords of the Romans were suitable for cutting and thrusting, whereas the long swords of the Caledonians were cumbersome and had no points.

The result was that the Caledonian front line was cut down, and the Romans advanced onto the higher ground. Meanwhile, the Roman cavalry had overthrown the chariots, and they joined in the general melée. The whole Caledonian force soon retreated to nearby woods, but Agricola ordered his men to make a ring around the woods, and the killing continued. Eventually the Caledonians took to flight, and they were pursued and slaughtered until nightfall. Next day, the Romans found the whole area deserted, with an eerie silence on the mountain range, and Agricola took his army slowly through all the adjacent territories to over-awe the tribes. He had already sent his fleet around the north of Scotland to show his power to all and sundry, and he was now poised for the total conquest of the island. Luckily for the peoples of Britain, however, the new Emperor Domitian was jealous of Agricola's success and had him recalled immediately to Rome.

Reconstruction of Celtic spears based on Danebury finds, also from Museum of the Iron Age, Andover, Hampshire.

Efforts by the Romans to get the Caledonian tribesmen to enlist in their army were unsuccessful, and within some years a new resurgence of these tribesmen took place. They attacked many of Agricola's fortresses, forcing the Romans to abandon them, and then in 119 AD the Brigantes rebelled and massacred the Roman legion which was stationed at York. The Emperor Hadrian arrived two years later, bringing fresh troops, and he soon forced the Brigantes to surrender again. With three legions, he then commenced the building of the famous wall which stretches from Bowness to Wallsend and which, with its periodic fortresses, provided a barrier against further raids from the north. In 142 AD, under orders from the Emperor Antoninus, the frontier was doubled with the construction further north of a turf-wall along the line of Agricola's old fortresses from the Firth of Forth to the Firth of Clyde.

Although these structures were an encumbrance to the Caledonians, they did not

Reconstruction of Celtic charioteer's tomb, with weapons and jewellery laid near the body.

prevent raiding altogether, and by 155 AD the Romans had begun to withdraw from the Antonine Wall. A decade later Hadrian's Wall was confirmed as the real frontier. In 181 AD the Caledonians stormed the great wall and killed the Roman commander there, causing the Emperor Commodus to send a hardened general, Ulpius Marcellus, against them. He drove the raiders back, but his successor Clodius Septimius Albinus became embroiled in the Imperial power-struggle and in 197 AD took the legions across to Gaul to have himself proclaimed Emperor there. He was defeated by Septimius Severus, but the Caledonians were emboldened by the departure of the backbone of the Roman army. They joined with the Maeatae tribe near Hadrian's Wall and began to ravage the area, but the Emperor Severus himself arrived in 208 AD with a massive army and pushed them north as far as Aberdeen. They put up stiff guerrilla resistance, however, causing

A slab to measure distance on the Antonine Wall at Bridgeness, West Lothian, Scotland. The wall was constructed by the Roman legions in 142 AD to hinder Pictish raids.

heavy casualties to the Romans, and the fighting continued even after Severus had retired to York, where he died in 211 AD.

By that time the Roman Empire was being threatened on a wider front by Germanic peoples, such as the Franks who burst into northern Gaul, the Burgundians who crossed the Main into eastern Gaul, and the Alemanni who ravaged northern Italy. Then, for the first time, Germanic tribes such as the Franks and Saxons began to raid the coast of Britain. In 286 AD, to counter these, a new man was appointed commander of the Roman fleet in the Channel, with instructions to protect the coasts of Gaul and Britain. He was of the tribe known as the Menapii, in north-eastern Gaul , and his name was Carausius. The Latin sources say that he was of humble origin and was at first a sea-pilot, but that he rose quickly through the ranks of the Roman army. Operating from his headquarters at Gessoriacum (modern Boulogne), Carausius patrolled the Channel and stopped the raids, but suspicion soon fell on him of being in collusion with the pirates and expropriating some of their loot.

He was condemned to death by the Emperor Maximian, but crossed to Britain and—with the help of the Roman legions there—proclaimed himself ruler of the island. In 289 AD Maximian set out for Britain to suppress him, but the Emperor's fleet was damaged by a storm and scattered by the able seamen of Carausius. Maximian and his fellow-Emperor Diocletian had little choice but to leave Carausius to his own devices, and he proclaimed himself the third Emperor and had coins struck with his name 'Marcus Aurelius Carausius' on them. In 292 AD, however, the Romans retook Gessoriacum, confining Carausius's power to Britain. As he made preparations to defend his position, he was murdered by his ambitious lieutenant Allectus. Three years later, the new western Emperor Constantius landed in Britain and defeated Allectus, thus restoring the island fully to the Roman fold.

Constantius made his headquarters at York, from where in 306 AD he began successful campaigns against the raids of the Caledonians or 'Picti' in the north and the Irish or 'Scotti' in the west. He died in the same year at York, and his son, Constantine, was proclaimed Emperor

there. It was this Constantine who made Christianity the official religion of the Empire. In Britain he instituted two new commands specifically designed to repulse raiders — one was the Dux Britanniarum function was to repulse the Caledonians and Irish in the north and west, and the other was the Comes Litori whose function was to defend the eastern and southern shores against the Saxons. Ultimately, both commands failed in their tasks. The first failure was in 368 AD, when the Caledonians over-ran York and swarmed southwards. The Roman commander Theodosius was sent from Gaul, and he broke up advance bands of the raiders near London. In the following year, he invaded Scotland, ravaged the countryside there, and restored Hadrian's Wall.

His campaign was continued by his successor Magnus Clemens Maximus, a Spaniard who had married a Briton wife. Having stabilised the northern border, this Maximus took his legions with him to Gaul in 383 AD in a bid to obtain the whole Empire for himself. He defeated an official Roman army at Paris, and set up his headquarters at Trier. He ruled as Emperor over Britain, Gaul, and Spain until he was defeated and put to death near Venice in 388 AD by the Emperor Theodosius, son of the man who had rebuilt Hadrian's Wall. The Wall itself was soon breached again from the north, however, and, with increasing raids by Saxons, Angles and Jutes in the south-east, Roman power in Britain was finally coming to an end.

The raids from the west at this period were very significant. Ireland had been untouched by the Roman legions, and a Celtic culture flourished there. It is not clear when the Bronze Age inhabitants of Ireland had been conquered or assimilated by the Celts in their westward expansion, but all the evidence is that the country had been fully Celticised from the late centuries BC. Ptolemy's geography, from the 2nd Century AD, gives several population names from the east coast of Ireland which indicate that some groups had only recently been settled there. These included the well-known Brigantes; the Coriondi, corresponding to tribes in Britain called the Corionototae and Coritani; and also the Monaqi, which designation seems similar to the placename Manavia for the Isle of Man and perhaps even to the population-name Menapii of Belgic Gaul.

The tribes inhabiting the rest of Ireland were no doubt descended from earlier Celtic settlers. The most powerful of these at an early date were the Iverni (better known from the later form of their name, Érainn), who were splitting into various regional groups such as the Dáirine, Ulaidh, Osraighe, and Uaithne. In or about the 2nd Century AD, a tribe known as Laighin or Gaileoin — who had some connections with the Brigantes in Britain—came to prominence in much of the country. From the 4th Century AD onwards the power of the Laighin shrunk to their original eastern areas, whereas two other groups came to dominate — the Connachta in much of the northern half of Ireland and the Eoghanacht in the southern half.

Irish Groups Invade The West Coast Of Britain

As the Roman control of Britain weakened, Irish groups began to settle in western Scotland and in the Isle of Man, thus bringing their dialect of Celtic to these areas. They also raided and settled in Wales — where the Lleyn peninsula preserves the name of the Laighin from Ireland. In time, the Connachta came to be the greatest of Irish raiders on the west coast of Britain. It was probably these who were referred to in an eulogy in which the brilliant Roman general, Stilicho, was praised for saving Britain in 399 AD 'when the Scot mobilised all Ireland, and the ocean was churned to foam by his hostile oars'. Native Irish literary sources refer to a semi-legendary king of the Connachta called Eochu, who had the sobriquet Muighmheadhon (literally 'lord of slaves'), and we read that among those taken by him in a raid on Britain was a girl called Cairenn. This is an Irish corruption of the Latin name Carina, and we read that the girl became the mother of Eochu's famous son Niall. When he came to manhood, Niall rescued her from servility and demanded recognition for her as a noblewoman.

Niall is described in early Irish literature as carrying out several great raids on the British coast, and he is said to have been killed on one such raid by a man of the Laighin, whom he had exiled to Britain. This happened in or about the year 454 AD. Legendary accounts state that his warriors brought his body home, and when attacked on their way they raised it aloft in the belief that Niall's reputation would weaken the spirit of the enemy. It was apparently on one of these raids into Britain that St Patrick was captured as a youth and first brought into Ireland. The raid on which he was taken was definitely a large one, for the saint himself states that thousands of people were taken. It is curious to consider that Ireland, the last Celtic country which Christianity reached, was converted, not through the power of Rome, but indirectly through the efforts of one of the last great Iron Age warriors.

The memory of great feats performed in ancient wars survived among later generations of Celts, and echoes of such can be traced in the mediaeval Irish and Welsh literatures. It is, for instance, possible that the Welsh tale of the raid on Ireland by the legendary super-king Bran, which caused his death, derives from lore preserved by the Belgae of the great raid on Delphi by Brennos. More definite are the Welsh accounts of Caswallawn, son of Beli Mawr, who— in the legend of his driving the Romans from Britain—surely represents the Cassivelaunus who opposed Julius Caesar. Caswallawn is represented as the owner of a great horse called Meinlas, which the Romans gave to him in return for permission to set foot in Britain, and this might reflect an actual gift given by Caesar to the historical king.

The career in the 4th Century AD of the imperial pretender Maximus is reflected in the story of Maxen Wledic who dreamt of meeting a beautiful lady in a wondrous land, and who on waking sent

his men in search of that place. She was found in Britain, and he went there and married her. He lost his empire in the process, however, and regained it only through the help of his wife's brothers, one of whom he settled in new territory in Brittany. This reflects the actual settlements in Brittany by refugees from the Anglo-Saxon invasion of Britain in the 5th and 6th Centuries, which brought a Celtic language back to the Continent. This language, Breton, was to be the only variant of Celtic to survive on the whole Continental land-mass.

Finally, the much-discussed origins of the legendary King Arthur, which name comes from a Romanised Celtic form Artorius, must be connected to battles fought by a type of post-Roman Dux Britanniarum or Comes Litoris against the Anglo-Saxons in the early 6th Century AD.

Mediaeval Irish literature is the richest of all in epical lore, and here too there are ancient echoes. These are most clearly identified in the numerous stories concerning the mythical Fionn mac Cumhaill and his band of young warriors called Fianna, which have as their source archaic Celtic traditions of young men's societies. Rumours of the deeds of Carausius must have reached Ireland in the 3rd Century AD, and these could subsequently have contributed to stories of the mythical Cú Roi, a great seafarer who fights many battles abroad and is treacherously killed. Last, and by no means, least is the super-hero of mediaeval Irish epic, Cú Chulainn, a stupendous fighter in a war-chariot bristling with weapons whose appearance becomes horrid in the frenzy of battle. His alias is Setanta, which parallels the name of the Setantii, a tribe allied to the Brigantes in Britain. There is no evidence for the war-chariot in Ireland, and so it is likely that the lore of Cú Chulainn originated with refugees from the wars of the Brigantes against the Roman legions. Descriptions of this Cú Chulainn in Irish literature, indeed, seem to encapsulate all the fierce drama which surrounded the Celtic warriors in their courageous but often futile battles in the Europe of long ago.

ABOVE: Hill-fort, dating from about 500 BC, at Maiden Castle, Dorset, England. It would have been occupied by one of the earliest large groups of Celts in Britain. Note the favoured high ground, which would make it suitable for defence.

RIGHT: Dún Aonghusa, the great fortress on Inishmore, one of the Aran Islands off the coast of Co. Galway. It overlooks a steep cliff-face, and was probably constructed during the early centuries AD. Defence was obviously the principal concern, as it is surrounded by three stone walls, and has a stone chevaux-de-frise encircling the second wall. The site may also have had a ritual function.

APPENDIX:
ANCIENT CELTIC PEOPLES

The following is a table of the principal Celtic peoples in or about the beginning of the 1st Century BC, based on the available reports of their locations and the forms of their names given in Latin and Greek sources. It can be assumed that the various groups were an amalgam between the general spread of Celtic groups from their original habitat north-east of the Alps and the influence of the three great Celtic strongholds in the 5th Century BC in the areas of the Marne, Moselle and western Bohemia. The most likely paradigm is, in fact, the radiating out of peoples and cultures from these three stronghold-areas, joining with less developed Celtic groups and subsuming other indigenous peoples and cultures in the process. Thus the principal influence on our Regions 1 and 2 (Central and North-West Gaul) would have been from the Marne; Region 3 (Belgic Gaul) would have had the Moselle as catalyst; while Regions 4 and 5 (South-East Gaul and the Danube) would have combined influences from the Marne and Bohemia. The subsuming of other peoples and cultures, which must have been part of the process from the beginning, is perhaps easiest to envision in the secondary regions of Celtic expansion, such as Britain, Ireland, Iberia, Italy, Eastern Europe and Asia Minor.

REGION 1	CENTRAL GAUL	AREAS OF FURTHER EXPANSION:
REGION 2	NORTH-WEST GAUL	BRITAIN, IRELAND, IBERIA, ITALY, EASTERN EUROPE
REGION 3	BELGIC GAUL	AND ASIA MINOR
REGION 4	SOUTH-EAST GAUL	
REGION 5	THE DANUBE	

ALPHABETICAL LIST OF CELTIC PEOPLES
(followed by region numbers or names)

Abrincatui (2)
Aduatici (3)
Aedui (4, Italy)
Aegosages (E.Europe/
    Asia Minor)
Allobroges (5)
Ambarri (4)
Ambiani (3)
Ambidrava (5)
Anares (1, Italy)
Ambisonti (5)
Ambivariti (3)
Andecavi/Andes (2)
Andes/Andecavi (2)
Aravisci (5)
Arecomici (5)
Armorici (2)
Arevaci (Iberia)
Arverni (1)
Atocini (5)
Atrebates (3, Britain)
Aucii (Ireland)
Aulerci (2, 4, Britain, Italy)
Baiocasses (2)
Batavi (3)
Belendones (Iberia)
Belgae (1, 3, Ireland)
Belgic tribes (Britain)

Belli (Iberia)
Bellovaci (3)
Berones (Iberia)
Bituriges (1)
Bodiontici (5)
Boii (1, 4, 5, Italy, Asia
    Minor)
Brannovices (4)
Brigantes (Britain, Ireland)
Cadurci (1)
Caeroesi (3)
Caletes (2)
Carni (5)
Carnutes (2)
Carpi (5)
Carvetii (Britain)
Caturiges (5)
Catuvellauni (1, Britain)
Cavares (4)
Celtiberi (Iberia)
Celtici (Iberia)
Cenomani (2, Britain, Italy)
Ceuleni/Cualainn (Ireland)
Ceutrones (5)
Condrusi (3)
Connachta (Ireland)
Consoranni (4)
Convenae (4)

Coriondi/Cuirinn (Ireland)
Corionototae (Britain)
Coritani (Britain)
Cornovii (Britain)
Cruitheni/Priteni (Ireland)
Cualainn/Ceuleni (Ireland)
Cuirinn/Coriondi (Ireland)
Darini (Ireland)
Decantae (Britain)
Deceangli (Britain)
Dematae (Britain)
Diablintes (2)
Dobunni (Britain)
Dumnonii (Britain, Ireland)
Durotriges (Britain)
Dáirine (Ireland)
Eburones (3)
Eburovices (2)
Eceni/Iceni (Britain)
Eoghanacht (Ireland)
Érainn (Ireland)
Esuvii/Sagii (2)
Feldubhair/Weldobri
>(Ireland)
Fir Domhnainn (Ireland)
Fir Monach (Ireland)
Fir Bolg (Ireland)
Féni (Ireland)

Gabali (1)
Gaileoin/Laighin (Ireland)
Galatae (see Gauls)
Galati (Asia Minor)
Gallaeici (Iberia)
Galli (see Gauls)
Gauls (1, Italy, Iberia)
Gododdin (Britain)
Gotini (5)
Helvetii (5)
Iceni /Eceni (Britain)
Insubres (4, Italy)
Insubres (Italy)
Iverni (Ireland)
Laighin/Gaileoin (Ireland)
Latobici (5)
Lemavi (Iberia)
Lemovices (1)
Leuci (3)
Lexovii (2)
Libici/Libui (Italy)
Libui/Libici (Italy)
Lingones (4, Italy)
Lusitani (Iberia)
Lusones (Iberia)
Manapii (Ireland)
Mandubii (4)
Marne Celts (1, Britain)

Mediomatrices (3)
Medulli (1)
Meldi (3)
Memini (4)
Menapii (3)
Monaqi (Ireland)
Morini (3)
Namnetes (2)
Nantuates (5)
Nervii (3)
Nitiobroges (1)
Novantae (Britain)
Ordovoci (Britain)
Osi (5)
Osissmii (2)
Osraighe (Ireland)
Paemani (3)
Parisii (1, Britain)
Petrocorii (1)
Pictavi (1)
Picti (Britain)
Pictones (1)
Priteni/Cruitheni (Ireland)
Quariates (5)

Rauraci (5)
Redones (2)
Regnes (Britain)
Remi (3)
Rhacatae (5)
Ruteni (1)
Sagii/Esuvii (2)
Saluvii/Salyes (4)
Salyes/Saluvii (4)
Santones (1)
Scordisci (5)
Sedunes (5)
Segni (3)
Segovellauni (4)
Segusiavi (4)
Selgovae (Britain)
Senones (1, Italy)
Sequani (4)
Setantii (Britain)
Silures (Britain)
Silvanectes (3)
Sobhairce/Soborgii
    (Ireland)
Suessatani (Iberia)

Suessiones (3)
Taurisci (5)
Tectosages/Volcae (1, 5,
    Asia Minor)
Tigurini (5)
Titti (Iberia)
Tolistoboii (Asia Minor)
Treveri (3)
Tricasses (1)
Tricastini (4)
Tricorii (4)
Trinovantes (Britain)
Trocmi (Asia Minor)
Tulingi (5)
Turolenses (Iberia)
Turoni (1)
Uaithne (Ireland)
Ulaidh (Ireland)
Uluti (Ireland)
Unelli (2)
Vaccaei (Iberia)
Vadicasses (3)
Vasates (1)
Veldrobi (Ireland)

Veliocasses (2)
Vellavi (1)
Venelli (2)
Veneti (2)
Veni (Ireland)
Veniscones (Britain)
Veragri (5)
Verbigeni
Vertacori (4)
Vettones (Iberia)
Viberi (5)
Viducasses (2)
Vindelici (5)
Viromandui (3)
Vivisci (1)
Vocontii (4)
Volcae/Tectosages (1, 4, 5,
    Asia Minor)
Votadini (Britain)
Volciani (Iberia, Ireland)
Weldobri/Feldubhair
    (Ireland)

R E G I O N   1   –   C E N T R A L   G A U L

The population groups in this region (which became essentially France) were mostly descended from a mixture of the Marne Celts and of other Celts who had long been settled north-west of the Alps.

One of the most celebrated groups of central Gaul were the Senones ('vanquishers'), who occupied the banks of the Yonne, and whose capital was called Agedincum (now Sens). A branch of them settled in Italy (see below). Their clients in France were the Parisii ('effective people', or perhaps worshippers of the 'effective' deity), whose centre was Lutecia (now Paris). Also dependent on the Senones were the Tricasses ('very strong ones'), who left their name on Troyes, and the Catuvellauni ('battle-superiors'), a branch of the Belgae who had their chief centre at Durocatalaunum (now Chalonge).

To their south were the Bituriges ('kings of the world'), who were—as their name indicates—a very important people. They were reputedly the leading tribe in the federation which sent the Celtic invaders into Italy and towards the east in the 4th Century BC. Their centre was Avaricum (modern Bourges), and their name survives as that of the department of Berry. A sub-group of the Bituriges, called Vivisci, had settled far to the south-west of there, and had as their centre Burdigala (now Bordeaux).

West of the Bituriges, on both banks of the Loire, were the Turoni ('the energetic ones'), who have given their name to Tours, where their chief fortress was.

Below the Turoni were the Pictavi or Pictones (perhaps meaning 'bad-tempered ones'), who have left their name on the department of Poitou, and who had their chief town at Limonum (now Poitiers).

Further south again, the Lemovices ('elm-conquerors') have left their name on the department of Limousin, and their capital was the origin of modern Limoges.

The most powerful group in all this region in later times were the Arverni (perhaps 'alder-guardians'), south of the Bituriges and in the modern department of Auvergne, which preserves their name. The principal centre of the Arverni was modern Gergovie, and they later founded another capital further north called Avernos (now Clermont). One of their client peoples were the Vellavi ('superior ones') on their southern flank, whose towns were Ruessio (now Saint-Paulien) and Anicium (now Le Puy). The Gabali ('capturers'), to the south of these again, in the Cévennes, were also clients of the Arverni, their chief town being Anderitum (now Javols).

The Ruteni ('red ones', referring to battle), whose capital was Segodunum (now Rodez, in the modern department of Aveyron) were further clients. Westward again, the Cadurci ('battle-boars') were also under the sway of the Arverni. Their capital was called Divona ('the goddess', now Cahors).

To the west of the Cadurci—in the modern department of Dordogne—were the Petrocorii ('four squadrons'), whose chief town was Vesunna (now Vésone).

The Santones (possibly 'select ones') have left their name on the area of Saintonge, north of Bordeaux. They had Mediolanum ('middle plain') for their capital somewhere in that area.

The Celtic presence beyond the Garonne was sporadic, most of the inhabitants being of Iberian stock. Most powerful of the Celtic groups there were the Nitiobroges ('owners of territory'), who were settled on both banks of the Garonne and whose capital was Aginnum (now Agen).

To the west of them were the Vasates ('pillagers'), whose

chief town was Cossium (now Bazas); while the Medulli ('mead-drinkers') gave their name to the peninsula of Médoc.

The Carnutes ('worshippers of the horned deity') were situated west of the River Seine, with Autricum (now Chartres) as their capital and Cenabum (now Orleans) as their commercial centre. Their territory was regarded in the 1st Century BC as the centre of all Gaul, and the periodic general assembly of Gaulish druids is reported to have taken place within it—in the area between Sully and Saint-Benoit-sur-Loire.

West of them, in the modern departments of Sarthe and Mayenne, were the very powerful Aulerci ('exiles'). Their principal group were the Cenomani ('those far removed'), whose chief town was Vindumun (now Celmans). Another section of them had the name Eburovices ('boar-conquerors') whose settlement was called Mediolanum (now Vieil-Évreux). The Sagii ('seekers'), also known as Esuvii ('people of Esus' – a deity whose name meant 'lord'), were connected with these Eburovices, and they occupied the major part of the department of Orne. Their town was known as Noviodunum ('new fortress', now Sées). The smallest group of the Aulerci were the Diablintes ('untiring ones'), whose town was also called Noviodunum (now the village of Jublains in the north of Mayenne).

In the south of this region, towards the banks of the Loire, were the Andes or Andecavi ('great strikers'), whose chief town was later called Angers from their name. Some of these, in league with the Cenomani, were involved in the invasion of north Italy.

Between the Andes and the Atlantic to the west were the Namnetes (perhaps 'enemies'), whose centre was Condevincon (now Nantes).

North of the Andes, in the area of Morbihan, were the Veneti ('tribesmen'), with their centre called Darioritum ('oak-ford', now known from their name as Vannes).

The Redones ('[chariot]drivers') were in the modern department of Ille-et-Vilaine, their capital being Condate (now known from their name as Rennes).

The people in the far north-west, in modern Finistère, were the Osissmii ('the furthest ones'). Their centre was Vorgium (apparently modern Carhaix-Plouguer).

In the extreme north, in the Cotentin Peninsula of modern Normandy, were the Unelli or Venelli ('tribesmen'). Their centre was Cosedia (now Coutances), and their principal port was Coriovallum (now Cherbourg). A southern branch of the Unelli were known as the Abrincatui (perhaps 'springers into battle'), from whom comes the placename Avranches.

Further east along the Atlantic coast were the Baiocasses (perhaps 'agile strikers'), whose town became known from their name as Bayeux, and their relatives the Viducasses ('agile woodsmen'), with their town of Aragenuae (now Vieux). Another people of this group, the Veliocasses or Caletes ('brave ones'), were settled on the east bank of the Seine. Their centre was Rotomagus (now Rouen), and

their port was Caracotinum (now Harfleur). It is possible also that the Tricasses of Troyes (see Senones above) and the Vadicasses near Nancy (see Leuci below) were of the same basic stock.

Situated between the Baiocasses and Viducasses on the one hand and the Veliocasses on the other – in the western elbow of the Channel and the Seine – were the Lexovii ('slope-people'), whose centre was Noviomagus ('new market', now Lisieux).

The tribes which formed the confederation of Belgae would appear to have derived from the ancient Celtic rulers of the Moselle Valley. The appellation 'Belgae' itself had a meaning such as 'raging' and was probably one of the euphuisms which the Celts liked to use for themselves as warriors.

The Remi ('the premier ones') occupied the northern parts of the modern departments of Marne and Aisne. Their capital was Durocortorum (now Reims), and they had another stronghold called after a leading Celtic deity viz. Lugudunum ('fortress of Lugus', now Laon).

The Suessiones were closely related to the Remi. They occupied most of the department of Aisne, and their capital was at Soissons. Their name possibly meant 'worshippers of the good Esus', Esus being a Celtic god (see Esuvii above). Among their dependent peoples were the Meldi ('thunderbolts'), whose town became Meaux, and the Silvanectes (perhaps 'forest-dwellers'), whose town became Senlis.

To the west of the Suessiones, occupying the modern department of Oise, were the Bellovaci ('war-slayers'), whose capital was at modern Beauvais. Their name suggests that they were very effective fighters, and their stronghold was Bratuspantium.

North of the Suessiones were the Ambiani ('those astride the water'), in the modern department of Somme. Their capital was Samarobriva ('bridge on the Samara', now Bray-sur-Somme), taking its name from that of the river.

East of the Ambiani were the Viromandui ('men-crushers'), whose centre later came to be known from their name as Vermand.

Further north were the Atrebates ('inhabitants'), whose centre was Nemetacus ('sacred place', now Arras).

In the centre and west of the modern department of Pas-de-Calais were the Morini ('sea-people'), whose centre was Tarvanna (now Thérouanne). Their chief port was Bononia (now Boulogne-sur-mer), through which the Belgae maintained contact with Britain.

The Menapii ('waterside-people') were a numerous Belgic people of the far north, inhabiting coastal parts of modern France, Belgium and Holland from Calais as far as the Rhine. Their territory bordered on that of the powerful Germanic tribe, the Batavi, in the east. Their chief centre was the origin of the town of Cassel, south of Dunkerque. One of their foundations was – like several other Celtic ones – known as the 'fortress' of the deity Lugus, viz. Lugudunum (now

Leiden). Another of their towns was Noviomagus ('new market', now Nijmegen).

South of the Menapii were the Nervii ('people of Nerios' – Nerios being a Celtic god of strength). They were reputedly the bravest of all the Belgae. The territory of the Nervii covered the plain of Belgium as far as the Sambre, and the modern department of Nord in France. Their centre was Bagacum (now Bavai). A northern branch of them, next to the Menapii, were called Ambivariti, and from them probably comes the name of the town of Antwerp.

The Eburones ('boar-hunters'), a small but hardy group, were south of the Nervii, in the forest of Ardenne. Other groups in this area were the Condrusi, Caeroesi, Paemani, Segni and Aduatici. The latter called their centre Aduatuca, and it later became known as Tungros (now Tongres). This placename reflects the appellation Tungri given to the Germanic tribes of the region, showing how close in contact the Celts of the area were to these tribes.

The most powerful of all the Celtic peoples of this area were the Treveri ('ferrymen'), who occupied the Moselle valley as far as the Rhine (encompassing the north of the modern Moselle department in France, Luxembourg, and the Rheinland area of modern Germany). The original name of their capital, on the river Moselle, is lost, but the place later became known in French as Trèves and in German as Trier.

A related group, called the Mediomatrici, were to the south of the Treveri. Their name meant 'between the mothers' (the 'mothers' referring to the goddesses of the rivers Moselle and Seille. Their capital was Divodurum ('divine stronghold', now Metz), and they had another important town on the Meuse called Verodunum (now Verdun).

Furthest south of the Belgae, stretching to the source of the river Meuse and to the borders of the territory of the Lingones, were the Leuci ('bright ones'). Their centre was Tullum (now Toul). They had a sub-group, or client-people, called Vadicasses.

REGION 4 – SOUTH-EAST GAUL

The groups in this region were probably an amalgam of the ancient rulers in the Marne with the Celts of the Danube.

The principal people here were the Aedui ('burners' or perhaps worshippers of a deity called Aedos, meaning fire), who occupied the modern department of Saône-et-Loire. Their chief centre was Bibracte ('beaver-place', now Mont-Beuvray, west of Autun). The Insubres, who invaded Italy, were a branch of the Aedui. The Aedui had several client peoples – including the Mandubii ('tramplers') on their northern border; the Brannovices ('frenzied conquerors'), a branch of the Aulerci, between the Loire and the upper Yonne; the Segusiavi ('victorious ones') to the south near Lyons; and the Ambarri, meaning 'those around the Arar – the Arar being the river Saône.

To the north of the Aedui – in the modern department of Haute-Marne – were the Lingones ('springers'), whose centre is now called Langres. A branch of them settled in Italy (see below).

Between the Saône and the Jura were the Sequani, who had come from the basin of the Seine, and had the name of that river (Sequana, i.e. 'spouting lady') attached to them. Their chief centre was Vesontio (now Besancon).

To their south were several small groups. The Vertacori inhabited the plateau between the Isère and Drac rivers, the Segovellauni were on the western bank of the Rhône, while the Tricastini had their centre at Senomagus ('old market', now Senos). The Vocontii ('double warriors') inhabited the mountainous area to the east of these.

The Cavares ('giants') inhabited the modern department of Vaucluse, and had the towns of Arausio (now Orange), Avenio (now Avignon) and Cabellio (now Cavaillon). A branch of these Cavares, called Memini, had the town of Carpentorate ('chariot course', now Carpentras).

Further south, along the banks of the river Durance and reaching almost as far as Arles, were the Saluvii or Salyes ('sea-coast dwellers'). These were just north of the strong Greek colony of Marseilles. The countryside east of that, along the Mediterranean coast, was inhabited by Ligurean peoples. This whole area, of course, became the 'Provincia' of the Romans.

For Volcae and Boii settlements in this area, see below.

Two other Celtic groups were settled, apparently by the Romans, in the Pyrenees – the Convenae ('companions'), whose centre was called Lugudunum (now Saint-Bertrand-de-Comminges); and the Consoranni ('associates'), whose centre was Austria (now Saint-Lizier).

REGION 5 – THE DANUBIAN CELTS

The Allobroges ('those from another territory') inhabited the area encompassed by the modern departments of Savoy and Dauphiné, as well as the adjacent area of south-western Switzerland. The vastness of their territory indicates how much land they had in fact taken over. Their centres were Vienna on the Rhône (now Vienne) and Genava (now Geneva).

To their south were the Caturiges ('battle kings'), who had the strong fortresses of Eburodunum (now Ebrun) and Brigantio (now Briancon). A further branch of them, the Quariates (whose name is congate with that of the Parisii (a branch of the Senones q.v.), account for the town of Queyras in the Alps.

Also in the western Alps were the Nantuates ('valley-people'), the Ceutrones ('forest-people'), and smaller groups such as the Veragri, Sedunes, Viberi, and Bodiontici.

Between the Jura and Lake Constance were settled the Helvetii ('demanders'), who had the forts of Aventicum (modern Avenches) and Vindonissa (modern Windisch). Their principal sub-tribe were the Tigurini ('claimers'), who crossed the Alps as part of the invasion by Germanic tribes in the late 2nd Century BC and may have left their name on Turin. Other tribes dependent on the Helvetii were the Rauraci, Tulingi, and Latobici. The Rauraci probably had moved south from the Ruhr, and one of their towns was Basilea (now Basel). The Tulingi ('good jumpers') and Latobici (perhaps 'marsh-dwellers') may have been branches of the Volcae in the area (see below).

The two most important Celtic peoples in the east were the Boii and the Volcae. These two seem to have worked in co-operation with each other from early times, and to have established a network of communities in the wide area running all along the foothills of the northern Alps. The Boii had the leading role towards the east, and the Volcae towards the west. The Boii (originally Bogii, 'strikers'), have left their name on Bohemia, and they played a leading part in the invasions of Greece, Italy, Thrace, and Asia Minor. They were the most powerful and influential people in the whole area of northern Austria. One of their major centres was Vindobona (now Vienna).

The Volcae ('wolves', meaning warriors), had the nickname Tectosages ('wealth-seekers'). They also played a leading role in Celtic raids and expansion, joining with the Boii in their adventures in the east. They pushed into the west also, for sections of them skirted the southern borders of Gaul and settled in that area in the 4th or 3rd Centuries BC, bringing a smaller group of Boii with them. This group of Boii settled almost as far west as Arcachon on the Atlantic coast. The Volcae themselves had three considerable settlements on that southern fringe of Gaul. One group of them, called Arecomici ('those near to allies'), had their centre at Nemausus (now Nîme); a second group, apparently mixed with the older Ligurean population, had the name Atacini and were at Narbonne; while the third, the Tectosages, controlled a large area around Toulouse.

There were several Celtic tribes along the Danube to the north of the Boii. These included the Vindelici of the Bavarian plateau on the southern side of the river, whose name may have meant 'subjects of Vindos'—this being the name of a deity, 'the bright one'. To their east, on the higher ground on the far side of the Danube, were the Osi ('high ones'). On the southern side of the river were groups such the Carpi (possibly 'allies') and the Rhacatae (possibly 'destroyers').

South of the Boii, in the area of east Austria and touching into modern Hungary and Croatia, were the Aravisci ('nearby friendly ones'), a name which they may have got from the Boii.

Groups of Celts who were settled in the southern Alps, stretching from Austria into Slovenia, were known as Taurisci. These were a new formation of disparate groups, which occurred after the failure of the invasion of Greece, and took their name from that of the mountain slopes in which they had settled. They divided themselves into Ambidrava (those who lived astride the river Drava) and Ambisonti (those who lived astride the river Isonta). Their capital was called Noreia, from which the area became known as Noricum.

Further south, the Carni ('followers of the horned one', i.e. a deity) controlled a wide area in the south-eastern Alps and modern Slovenia. South of them again, another new formation of Celtic peoples had resulted from the failed expedition to Greece. These, the Scordisci, had taken their name from Mount Scordus, and they called their chief centre Singidunum (now Belgrade)

In the far north-east, isolated from the rest of the Celts, were the Gotini of Galicia (on the modern Polish-Slovak border). Their name seems to have meant 'stammerers', a

natural designation for a people long separated from their linguistic relatives.

BRITAIN

The earliest Celtic groups to settle in Britain were probably arriving soon after 500 BC. These would appear to have been 'Marne Celts' whose power was by that time well established on the English Channel. Some centuries later, Belgic tribes had spread into that part of northern Gaul, and some of these began to cross into Britain. By the beginning of the 1st century BC the Belgic groups had taken over most of the southern coast of Britain and had established themselves a good distance inland. As elsewhere in the Celtic world, there were many minor groups, but the major ones are here listed.

The Caledones ('hard-fighters') of the far north of Britain must have been descendants of an indigenous population, whom the Romans later called Picti. The name Caledones would have been applied to them by incoming Celts.

In the south-west of Scotland were the Selgovae ('hunters'), the Novantae ('energetic ones'), and a branch of the Dumnonii, a larger group of whom were in Devon and Cornwall (see below). In the south-east of Scotland, around the Firth of Forth, were a group known as Venicones ('tribesmen'). South of them were a group known as Corionototae ('people of the [fighting] corps'), who may have been related to the Coritani below. South again, on the modern Scottish-English border, were the Votadini ('those subject to the father' - a designation which probably refers to worship of the Celtic ancestor-deity). This was the tribe which later became known in Welsh as Gododdin.

The Brigantes ('Briganti people'—referring to the goddess Briganti, meaning 'the high one') were the most powerful people in the north of England. Their capital was at Isurium (now Aldborough in Yorkshire). To their north were the Carvetii ('deer-hunters'), who had their centre at Luguvalium (now Carlisle). To their west, on the coast of the Irish Sea, were the Setantii (perhaps Sedontii, 'those seated [in chariots]'). Both of these groups seem to have been clients of the Brigantes.

East of the Brigantes on the North Sea coast were the Parisii, whose name indicates that they were the same as the Parisii, a branch of the Senones in Gaul (q.v.). South of the these were the Coritani (perhaps Coriatani 'those of the [fighting] corps'), whose centre was at Ratae (now Leicester).

In north Wales were the Deceangli or Decantae (perhaps 'good borderers'); in central Wales the Ordovoces ('hammer-fighters'); and in south Wales the Dematae (perhaps 'sheep-people'), whose centre was Moridunum (now Carmarthen). The Silures (perhaps 'sowers in the earth') had a centre at Venta (Caerwent); and on the Welsh-English border were the Cornovii ('people of the horned one'—a deity). The Dobunni were in modern Gloucestershire, with a centre at Corinium (Cirencester)—their name has not been explained, unless it be connected with that of their southern neighbours, the Dumnonii.

These Dumnonii ('people of the deep' i.e. people far away) were in Devon and Cornwall, with their centre at Isca (now Exeter). To their east were the Durotriges ('stronghold-people'), with a capital at Durnovaria (now Dorchester).

Definitely Belgic were the Catuvellauni ('battle-superiors') of central England, the most powerful people in all of Britain. They appear to have originally been a branch of the Catuvellauni of Gaul, clients of the Senones (q.v.). Their capital was Verulamium (now St Albans).

The Iceni or Eceni ('people far away') were to their east in the area of The Wash, having their centre at Venta (now Caistor St Edmund). They seem also to have originally been a branch of a Gaulish people, the Cenomani, who were the leading group of the very powerful Aulerci.

The Trinovantes ('very energetic ones') were further south, with their capital of Camulodunum (now Colchester).

The Atrebates, a branch of the Belgic tribe with the same name (q.v.) were near the southern coast, in modern Hampshire, with their capital at Calleva (now Silchester). There may have been some Atrebates in Britain before Caesar's time, but their kingdom as such must have been established after this by Commius.

Finally, nearest to Gaul in the south-east of England were the Regnes ('stiff people' in the sense of being proud), with their centre at Noviomagus (now Chichester); and the Cantiaci ('border-people'), with their centre at Durovernum (now Canterbury).

IRELAND

The population groups of prehistoric Ireland are more obscure, and must be deduced from the corrupted references of the geographer Ptolemaeus in the 2nd Century AD, combined with native genealogies from a much later period, and some archaeological evidence. Since most of the Celts must have reached there from Britain, perhaps in the 4th Century BC at the earliest, one would expect to find similarities between some of the population-names in the two islands. There are a few such similarities, but not enough to clarify the picture. As in other areas, earlier populations must have been subsumed into the Celtic groups.

One of the most widespread population names was Iverni ('land-dwellers'). The dominant element in these people must have been one of the first Celtic groups to reach the island. They may have been the first of the Celts to adapt Temoria (Teamhair, in English 'Tara', in County Meath) as a sacred site of kingship. Sections of the Iverni came to be known by different names, and these lived in different parts of the country—for example, Iverni and Veldobri in the south; Ceuleni and Aucii in the east; Uluti, Darini, and Soborgii in the north; Autini in the west. The Uluti ('bearded ones') and the Darini ('fertile ones', probably named from a god Darios – 'he who fertilises') were the most powerful of these. The Uluti had the celebrated site of Isomnis (later Eamhain) in County Armagh as their sacred centre.

Groups called Dumnonii were in the Dublin area in the east and the Mayo area in the west. These must have been a branch of the Dumnonii who had crossed the sea from either Devon or the west coast of Scotland.

A group called Veni were also in the south. These might have been of the same original stock as the Veneti of Brittany, the Venelli of Normandy, and the Venicones of Scotland. Perhaps they had come from the Continental coast, or had come from Britain where they were once more widespread.

The south-east corner of the island has always been the principal area for the introduction of new elements into Irish life. It is not surprising, therefore, to find mention by Ptolemaeus of Brigantes, Coriondi, and Manapii in that area. The designation Brigantes is the most readily understood, for this strong Celtic group from Britain was located in a position to have an influence on the eastern part of Ireland.

The Coriondi echo the element 'corio' (meaning 'host' or 'army') which was frequent in Celtic placenames in Britain, as well as the tribal names Corionototae and Coritani also in Britain.

It is tempting to regard the Manapii (correct Irish form Monaqi) as a branch of the Belgic Menapii, but the parallel may be coincidental, as both names may mean simply 'dwellers by the water'. There are several indications that groups of Belgae did reach Ireland in prehistory, but the precise dates and places are difficult to decipher.

To judge by the name Fothadh later given to mythical characters, there may also have been a branch of the Votadini from Britain settled in Ireland. The presence of various newcomers from Britain in prehistoric Ireland seems to be evidenced by a designation by which a number of tribes were known. This, Cruitheni, comes from Priteni, a term used for the older pre-Belgic Celts inhabiting Britain.

The following are groups referred to in post-Christian Ireland who seem to have derived from some of the above-mentioned early people—Érainn, Dáirine, Ulaidh, Uaithne, and Osraighe from the Iverni; Fir Domhnainn from the Dumnonii; Fir Monach from the Monaqi; Fir Bolg (a general attribution for many tribes) from the Belgae. The Laighin ('lance-men', also known as Gaileoin), who had the great hill-fort of Ailinn in County Kildare as their centre, apparently derived from the Brigantes. Some group-names only survived as toponymics, e.g. Weldobri as Feldubhair, Ceuleni as Cualainn, Soborgii as Sobhairce, Coriondi as Cuirinn. The two leading septs in pre-mediaeval Ireland, the Connachta of Tara and the Eoghanacht of Cashel, may have been descendants of the Féni.

IBERIA

Celtic peoples from Gaul had reached the Iberian Peninsula by the 5th Century BC, probably passing over the western Pyrenees. From there they spread into the centre of modern Spain. Another Celtic invasion followed this, by groups whose names indicate that they were of Belgic extraction. These seem to have followed a similar route as their predecessors, and to have pushed the earlier Gaulish groups further into the Peninsula. In general, the Celts of Iberia were to a greater or less extent mixed with earlier populations.

In the north-west of the Peninsula were the people known as the Gallaeici ('Gaulish ones'), who have left their name on modern Galicia. Their chief centres were

Brigantium (now La Coruña) and Caladunum (now Calahorra). These included groups such as the Lemavi and Turolenses, both of whom may have originally belonged to the Lemovices and Turoni of Gaul.

To their south were the Vettones and Lusitani, who seem to have had an influential Celtic minority in their make-up; while in the south-west of the Peninsula were a group known simply as the Celtici ('Celtic people'), with a centre at Mirobriga (now Santiago do Cacém).

Furthest east of the Celts in the Peninsula—in the whole area of Zaragoza around the confluence of the rivers Jalón and Ebro — were a population to whom the Latin writers often referred specifically as Celtiberi. These were groups of Galli, Turolenses, and Lusones. Their presence is echoed by the placenames Gállego and Teruel, and they—like their namesakes in Galicia—must have been descended from the initial Gaulish incursions into Iberia. The Lusones, who bore an Iberian name, were nevertheless strongly Celticised. These 'Celtiberi' had important centres such as Contrebia (now Botorrita), Nertobriga (now Calatorao), Bilbilis (now Calatayud), and Segeda (now Belmonte).

Belgic groups had taken much of the Ebro valley. In the western part of that valley were the Berones (perhaps 'mountain-dwellers'), whose centre was Varia (now Varea, near Logroño), and the Belendones ('worshippers of Belenos' — a Celtic god of brightness). Along the mid-Ebro were the Suessatani, whose name echoes the Suessiones in Belgic Gaul.

The Vaccaei (perhaps 'slayers'), of Belgic origin, were very numerous, inhabiting the area between the rivers Duero and Tormes, with a centre at Cauca (now Coca). To their east, across the river Zapardiel, were the Arevaces ('those near to the Vaccaei'), whose centres were Numantia (now Garray) and Seguntia (now Sigüenza).

South of the Arevaci, as far as the river Jalón, were the Belli ('warriors'), with a centre at Arcobriga (now Arcos). On the southern side of the Jalón were the Titti (perhaps from the Celtic 'Teutae', meaning people), with a centre at Segobriga (now Cabeza del Griego).

ITALY

These groups invaded the north of Italy in the 4th Century BC, and the region inhabited by them was thus called Cisalpine Gaul. They belonged to tribes well known in the Celtic world north of the Alps. There is little doubt but that earlier peoples whom they displaced, such as Ligurians and Etruscans, continued to live side by side with these Celts in much of the region. Towards the end of the 3rd Century BC the Romans took over Cisalpine Gaul and displaced many of the Celtic settlers there.

At the foot of the western Alps were the Libici or Libui, apparently a branch of the Saluvii of southern Gaul. Between the Ticino and the Adda, were the Insubres, who had as their centre Mediolanum (now Milan). These Insubres were a branch of the Aedui. The Cenomani (who were a branch of the Aulerci) were on both sides of the river Oglio, as far as the Po, and their centres were Tridentum (now Trent), Brixia (now Brescia) and Bergomum (now Bergamo). In the rich lands south of the Po, as far as the river Renus, were a branch of the Boii, one of the most migratory of all the Celtic peoples. Their centres in Italy were Mutina (now Modena) and Bononia (now Bologna). East of them, as far as the Adriatic, were settled the branch of the Lingones who had crossed the Alps. Finally, south of the Renus and between the Appennines and Ancona, were the branch of the Senones who founded Sena Gallica (now Senigallia).

EASTERN EUROPE & ASIA MINOR

After the failed attack on Greece in the 3rd Century BC, some Celtic groups moved eastwards in search of better fortune. One section founded a kingdom in Thrace, which lasted for two or three generations until it was overthrown by the native Thracians in 193 BC. A group from there who became mercenaries were called Aegosages ('combat-seekers').

The settlement of Galatia in Asia Minor (in the centre of modern Turkey) lasted longer. There were three groups involved in this. The Tectosages had their capital at Ancyra (now Ankara); the Tolistoboii were to their west, with their capital at Pessinus; and the Trocmi were to their east, with a capital at Tavium. Here again we find the Volcae (Tectosages) and the Boii in association with each other, and there may indeed be a functional connection between the three names —Tectosages ('wealth-seekers'), Trocmi ('poor people'), and Tolistoboii (perhaps 'increasing Boii'). It is tempting to connect the designation Tolistoboii (written also as 'Tolostoboii') with the legendary treasure placed by the Tectosages in Lake Tolosa at Toulouse. Perhaps that lake got its name from such a treasure, and the Celts in Asia Minor may have preserved a tradition of the sharing out of treasure as a ritual which determined the relationships between different groups. We may speculate that this was part of the ritual at the Galatian sanctuary of Drynemeton, and the leaders of the three tribes could therefore have had the titles 'Tectosagis', 'Tolistos', and 'Trocus' respectively.

NOTES AND REFERENCES

CHAPTER 1

For tumuli and burials, see Filip, 19-20, 31-50; Cunliffe, 42-4, 52-6.

Word 'Celt': Hieronymus of Cardia, from Pausanius 1.3.5; Strabo 4.1.14; See Walde/Pokorny 1, 436-40; Falk/Torp, 82-4.

For hill-forts, see Cunliffe, 44, 61-4.

For wine, see Tierney, 248-9.

For metals, see Filip, 50-8; Walde/Pokorny 1, 4; T F O'Rahilly in Ériu 13, 119-20.

For the regions of Marne, Moselle, and Bohemia, see Cunliffe, 63-7.

Himilco: Dinan, 9-27; Powell, 21-2; Rankin, 2-8; Tierney, 193.

For Ierne, Albion, see O'Rahilly, 40-2, 385-7 and in Ériu 14, 7-28; J Pokorny in Ua Riain, 237-43; Rankin, 2-8; Powell, 21-4; Tierney, 195-6

For 'Pritani', see K Jackson in Wainwright, 158.

Hecataeus re Narbon: Dinan, 8-9.

Danube: Herodotus 2.33 and 4.49.

Descriptions of Celts: Aeschylus - see Dinan, 28-9; Ephorus — see Dinan, 44-5 and Tierney, 270; Aristotle, Politica 2.9.7 and *Ethica*
Nicomachea 3.7.7 and *Politica* 4.17.2; Posidonius in Diodorus Siculus 5.32.7; Plato, *Leges* 1.637.

Ambassadors to Alexander: Strabo 7.3.8; Arrian, *Anabasis Alexandri* I, 4-6.

Celts and aquatic disaster: Strabo 7.2,1; Pseudo-Aristotle, *Ethica Eudemia* III, 1.25; Nicolas of Damascus.

Fondness for war: Xenophon, *Hellenica* VII, 1.20, 31; Strabo 4.4.2.

Appearance and clothing: Diodorus Siculus 5.28, 30-1. For archaeological evidence of Celtic dress, see Filip, 34.

Eating and drinking: Athenaeus 4.36, 40; Diodorus Siculus 5.26, 28.

Duelling and fighting: Athenaeus 4.40; Silius Italicus 16.537; Florus 1.33; Strabo 3.4.18; Plutarch, *Sertorius*, 14.4; Valerius Maximus 2.6.11.

Carrion-crows: Silius Italicus 3.340-3; Aelian, *Natura Animali* 10.22. See also note to Chapter 2 on battle-raveness.

Social disposition: Caesar, *De Bello Gallico*, 6.23.9 and 6.11.2-5; Strabo 6.4.2.

Selection of war-leader: Strabo 4.4.1.

Brigandage: Caesar, *op cit*, 6.23. 5-9. For young men's societies in European antiquity, see Wikander.

Pytheas re sun: in Geminius, *Elementorum Astronomiae* V, 22.

For the oherworld island, see references in Graves 2, 132-5, 140-1.

Plutarch re island: *Moralia*, 419, 941.

Island in Loire: Posidonius in Strabo 4.4.6.

Senae: Posidonius in Pomponius Mela, *De Situ Orbis* 3.6. See O'Rahilly, 4-5.

Druids: Strabo, 4.4.4; Diodorus Siculus 5.31. For other Classical references to the druids, see Kendrick, 73-106, 212-221. See also Walde/Pokorny, 1, 293-4, 804-6; Piggott, 20-75; Le Rouz/Guyonvarc'h, 125-216; M J Enright in Ni Chatháin/ Richter, 219-27.

For goddesses, see Holder 1, 1239 and 2, 468-70 and 1, 1273-4; Dinan, 62-3; Vries, *passim.*

For gods, see Caesar, *op cit*, 6.18.1. See also Walde/Pokorny, 1, 772-3; Eliade 7, 198-200; E Windisch in *Irische Texte* 1, 463; Guyonvarc'h in *Ogam* 11, 284-5 and 12, 49; Vries, *passim.*

Praise-poets: Athenaeus 6.49; Diodorus Siculus 5.31. See also Dottin, 146-9; D Ward in *Journal of Indo-European Studies* 1, 127-44; Ó hÓgáin, 364-9.

For Celtic expansion, see Dinan, 10-13, 28-31; Filip, 51, 61. See also Whatmough, 9-85.

CHAPTER 2

Wine: Pliny the Elder 12.5; Livy, 5.33. See Cunliffe, 69.

Clusium story: Livy 5.33.

Illyrians tricked: Theopompus - see Dinan, 46-9.

Population explosion: Justinian 1. 24. 4. See Arbois de Jubainville, 248.

'Ver sacrum': Justinian 1.24.1-3. See Hubert, 119-20.

Ambicatus: Livy 5.34.

For ritual truth of kings, see Dillon, 16-18; Ó hÓgáin, 263-4.

Invasions of Italy: Livy 5.33-35; Polybius 2.17-18.

For Insubres settlement, see Cunliffe, 70-2.

Sack of Rome: Polybius 2.18; Livy 5.35-39, who places these events some years earlier, in 390 BC.

Other early wars with Romans: Livy 6.42 and 7.1-15, 22-26.

Manlius Torquatus: Livy 7.9-10.

Marcus Valerius: Livy 7.26.

Single combat before battle: Diodorus Siculus 5.29. See also Jackson (1964), 30-1.

For battle-raveness, see W M Hennessy in *Revue Celtique* 1, 32-5; Ross, 282-5, 313-8; Ó hÓgáin (1990), 307-9, 439. See also note to Chapter 1 re carrion-crows.

For Irish references to withdrawing after death of leader, see Jackson (1938), 73; Knott, 45-6; Binchy, 17.

War of 299-297 BC: Polybius 2.19.

War of 296-283 BC: Livy 10. 16-30; Polybius 2.19-20.

CHAPTER 3

For names of Boii and Volcae, see Lambert, 34-5, 44, 58.

Segovesus guided by birds: Justin 24.4.

Celtic tribes in eastern Europe: Strabo 7. 2. See also Hubert, 57-66; Rankin,14-20.

Philip's assassination: Diodorus Siculus16.94; Justin 9.6.

For Alexander and Celts, see note to Chapter 1, and also Dinan, 88-93; Hubert, 33-5.

Kings buy peace from Celts: Justin 24.4, apparently quoting Hieronymus of Cardia, who lived in the 4th-3rd Century BC - see Dinan, 92-3, 132-3.

Great raid on Macedonia and Greece and failed attack on Delphi: Pausanius 1.4 and 10.19-23; Justin 24.4-8; Diodorus Siculus 22.8-9.

For career of Ptolemaeus Ceraunus, see Lemprière, 571, 615-6.

For pseudonym 'Thunderbolt', see Holder 1, 374-84; O'Rahilly (1946), 43-71.

Sosthenes: Justin 24.5.12-13.

'Trimarcisia': Pausanius 10.19.

For suicide of Brennos, see Dinan, 130-1.

Soteria: Diodorus 22.3-5; Justin 24.4; Pausanius 1.4, 10.5-13. See Rankin, 97-100; Cunliffe, 82.

Tectosages and treasure: Justin 32.3; Strabo 4.1.13.

Identity of Brennos: Strabo V.1.12-3 states he 'is said by some to have been a Prausan, but neither am I able to state in regard to the Prausans where on earth they lived formerly'. See also Holder, 1, 520-4.

Antigonus Gonatas and banquet-trick: Justin 25.1-2.

Conquest of Thrace: Polybius 4.46; Justin 32.3.6. See Hubert, 42-61.

Tribute from Byzantines: Athenaeus 233-4. See Rankin, 188.

Cavaros: Polybius 4. 46-52 and 8.24.

For the word 'Gallus', see Walde/Pokorny 1, 539-40, 641.

Galati raids and settlements in Asia Minor: Justin 25.2; Pausanius

1.4 and 10.22, 30, 32; Livy 38.16. See Arbois de Jubainville, 84; Hubert, 45-6; Rankin, 192.

Galati at war with Syrians: Justin 25; Lucian, *Zeuxis*, 9-12. See Hubert, 46.

For 'galatika', see Hubert, 47; Rankin, 189.

Defeats by Pergamum: Livy 38.16-17; Pausanius 1.4 and 10.30-32. See also Hubert, 45-9; Ellis, 92-7.

Celtic mercenaries in Syria: Polybius 4. 48 and 5.53, 82.

Celtic mercenaries in Pergamum: Polybius 5.78, 111.

Massacre by Prusias: Polybius 5.111.

For central shrines, see Hubert, 232-3; Byrne, 58.

CHAPTER 4

Fighting tactics of mercenaries: Xenophon, *Hellenica* 7.1.

Drunkenness: Plato, *Leges*, 1.637.

Celtiberians: Posidonius in Strabo 3.3-4. See Cunliffe, 142-3.

Celtic mercenaries with Carthaginians: Livy 7.27 and 9.43. With Antigonas Gonatas: Trogus Pompeius, *Prologi*, 26 - see Hubert, 41-2. In Egypt: Pausanius 1.7.2; Callimachos, *Hymn to Delos*, 185-6 - see Hubert, 51.

Pyrrhus and Celtic mercenaries: Pausanius 1.13.2; Plutarch, *In Pyrrhum*, 26; Justin 25.3.

Celts desecrate tombs in Macedonia: Plutarch, *In Pyrrhum*, 26; Diodorus Siculus 22.12.

Celtiberian mercenaries in Sicily and Epirus: Diodorus Siculus 16.73; Polybius 2.5-7.

Revolt of mercenaries in Carthage: Polybius 1.66-88.

Hamilcar Barca and Celtiberi: Polybius 2.1; Livy 21.1-2; Diodorus Siculus 25.10; Appian 6.1 (4-5); Cornelius Nepos 22.4..

Hasdrubal builds Carthaginian power in Spain: Polybius 2.13; Livy 21.2.

War in Italy between Celts and Romans: Polybius 2.21-35.

Assassination of Hasdrubal: Livy 21.2.

Hannibal and Spain: Livy 21.5-15.

Roman envoys rejected by Celts: Livy 21.19-20.

Hannibal negotiates with Celts: Livy 21.23-24.

Boii and Insubres rebel in Italy: Livy 21.25-26.

Hannibal in Gaul: Polybius 3.34-46; Livy 21.26-32. Crosses the Alps: Polybius 3.47-55; Livy 21.32-37. In Italy: Polybius 3.56-11; Livy 21-30.

Hannibal and single combat of Celtic prisoners: Polybius 3.62; Livy 21.42-43.

Hannibal in disguise from Celts: Polybius 3.78; Livy 22.1.

Flaminius killed by Celt: Polybius 3.84; Livy 22.6.

Gauls and Celtiberians at Battle of Cannae: Polybius 3.114; Livy 22.46.

Boii ambush Roman army: Livy 23.24; Polybius 3.118.

Head-cult among the Celts: Diodorus Siculus 5.29.

Celtiberi defeat Hasdrubal: Livy 22.21.

Moenicaptus and Vismarus: Livy 24.42.

Indibilis and Mandonius: Livy 29.1-3; Appian 6.8 (37-9).

Single combat between Corbis and Orsua: Livy 28.21.

Celtiberian force arrive in Carthage and massacred by Scipio: Polybius 14. 7,11-16; Livy 30.7-8.

Battle of Zama: Polybius 15.5-15; Livy 30.29-35.

CHAPTER 5

War of 200 BC: Livy 31.2, 10, 21.

War of 193 BC: Livy 33.36-37, 35.11.

Murder of Boii nobleman: Livy 39.42.

War of 191 BC: Livy 36.39-40. See Hubert, 84-5; Ellis, 65.

Conquest of Galati by Romans: Polybius 21. 33-46; Livy 38.12-27, 45-48.

Ortagio: Polybius 22.21.

Galatian campaigns of 179-165BC: Polybius 24.14-15 and 25.2 and 29.22 and 30.1-3, 19, 28; Strabo 13; Justin 31, 34.

Galatian dependence on Rome: Polybius 30. 29-30.1.

Turdetani rebellion: Strabo 3.2.15; Livy 33.19, 25, 43-44.

Cato's campaign: Livy 34.8-21; Plutarch, Cato, 10-11; Appian 6.8 (39-41).

Battle of Toletum: Livy 35.7.

War of 181 BC: Livy 35.7; 40.30-33.

Battle of Manlian Pass: Livy 40.35-40.

War of 179 BC: Livy 40.47-50.

Policy of Gracchus: Appian 6.8 (43); Strabo 3.4.

Attack on Claudius: Livy 41.26.

Salendicos: Florus 2.16.

War against Nobilior: Livy, *Periochae* 47; Appian 6.9 (44-7).

Policy of Marcellus: Appian 6.9 (48-50).

Massacre of Lusitani: Appian 6.9 (52).

Viriathos: Appian 6.11-12 (61-74); Dio Cassius 22; Florus 2.16; Valerius Maximus 6.4; Livy 53-54; Valerius Maximus 6.4; Orosius 5.4. See also Lemprière, 719.

Funeral of Viriathos: Appian 6.12 (75).

Mancinus: Appian 6.13 (80-3); Cicero, *De oratore*, 1.40. See Lemprière, 382; Ellis, 52.

Siege of Numantia: Appian 6.14-15 (84-98); Orosius 5.7-7.

CHAPTER 6

Marseilles and Romans: Polybius 33.8-10; Livy, *Epitome* 61; Strabo 4.1.5; Florus 3.2; Diodorus Siculus 34.23. See Jullian 3, 7-37; Hubert, 144.

War of Romans against Allobroges and Arverni: Livy, *Epitome* 61; Florus 1.37; Orosius 5.13-14. See Jullian 3, 14-19.

Generosity of Lovernios: Athenaeus 4.37.

Defeat of Arverni: Livy, *Epitome* 61; Valerius Maximus 9.6; Florus 3.2; Orosius 5.14.

Cimbri and Celts: Strabo 7.2.2.

War of Cimbri and Teutones against Romans: Livy, *Epitome*, 67-68; Plutarch, *Marius*, 11-27; Florus 3.3. See Hubert, 103-111.

Celts with Spartacus: Caesar, *De Bello Gallico* 1.40; Florus 3.20; Appian 1; Plutarch, *Crassus* 8-11; Orosius 5.24.

Sertorius: Plutarch, *Sertorius*; Florus 3.22; Orosius 5.23

Conspiracy of Catalina: Sallust, *Catalina*; Suetonius, *Julius Caesar*, 14-17; Plutarch, *Caesar*, 7-8.

Anecdote of Caesar in Alps: Plutarch, *Caesar*, 11.

Ariovistus and Gauls: Caesar, *De Bello Gallico*, 1.30-31.

Boerebistas: Strabo 7.3.11; Jordanes, *Getica*, 11.67; Trogus Pompeius, *Prologi*, 32.10. See Jullian 3, 149-52; Hubert, 115; Cunliffe, 222-3, 314.

War of Helvetii: Caesar, *De Bello Gallico* [henceforth referred to as *BG*] 1.1-29.

Caesar's war with Ariovistus: *BG* 1.30-54.

War of Belgae: *BG* 2.1-33.

Rebellion in Alps: *BG* 3.1-6.

War in north-west Gaul: *BG* 3.7-19.

War in south-west Gaul: *BG* 3.20-27.

Caesar's campaign in north-east Gaul and Germany: *BG* 3.28-29 and 4.1-19.

Invasions of Britain by Caesar: *BG* 4.20-38 and 5.1-23.

Dumnorix: *BG* 1.3, 9, 17-20 and 5.6-7.

Rebellion of Indutiomarus and Ambiorix: *BG* 5.24-58 and 6.1-8, 29-44; Dio Cassius 40.

Rebellion of Vercingetorix: BG 7.1-90; Plutarch, Caesar, 27; Dio Cassius 40 and 41.1-3 and 43.19.4.

Resistance by Gutuator and Commius: Hirtius, *BG*, 8.1-49.

Slaughter of Galatian nobles: Appian 12.7 (46).

Deïotarus: Cicero, *Pro rege Deitaro*; Strabo 12; Dio Cassius 41.63 and 42.46 and 47.24, 28 and 48.33; Appian 12.17 (114).

CHAPTER 7

Romans take over Galatia: Dio Cassius 50.13 and 51.7 and 53.26. See Hubert, 88-9; Ellis, 106.

Celtic mercenaries in Judaea: Josephus, *Antiquitates*, 15.7.3 and 17.8.3

For Romanisation of Gaul, see King, 63-88.

Rebellions of Florus and Sacrovir: Tacitus, Annales, 3.40-46.

Invasion of Britain by Claudius: Dio Cassius 60.19-23; Suetonius, Claudius 17 and Vespasian 4.

Rebellion of Iceni and resistance of Caratacus: Tacitus, *Annales*, 12.31-37; Dio Cassius 61.33.3.

Rule of Didius: Tacitus, *Annales*, 12.40.

Nepos' boast and Suetonius' attack on Anglesey: *ibid*, 14.29-30.

War of Boudicca: *ibid*, 14.31-38; Dio Cassius 62.1-12.

Rebellion of Vindex: Dio Cassius 63.22-26.

Persecution of Helvetii: Tacitus, *Historiae*, 1.67-70.

Rebellion of Germans and Gauls: *ibid*, 1.12-5.24.

Brigantes war of 71 AD: *ibid*, 3.45.

Agricola's campaign in Britain: Tacitus, *Agricola*.

Hadrian's Wall, Antonine Wall, and continuing fighting: Dio Cassius 72.8-9 and 75.5; *Historia Augusta*; Lampridius, Commodus, 6.1-2 and 8.4-5 and 13.5. See Collingwood/ Myres, 120-160; Winbolt, 24-30; Todd, 103-181.

Carausius: Eutropius 9.14; Aurelius Victor, *Caesares*, 39; Eumenius, *Panegyrici*, 2.12 and 5.12. See Todd, 207-11.

Constantius to Theodosius: Eutropius 9.21-22. See Collingwood/Myres, 277-88.

Maximus: Zozimus 1.4; Theodoret 1.5. See Collingwood/Myres, 286-94.

For early Celtic Ireland, see O'Rahilly, 1-57.

Stilicho: Claudian, *De Bello Getico*, 404-418 and *Stilicho*, 2.247-255. See Todd, 236-7.

Niall: *Ériu* 4, 91-111; *Otia Merseiana* 2, 75-6, 84-92. See Byrne, 70-86; Ó hÓgáin, 322-4.

For comparison of Bran with Brennos, see J T Koch in *Cambridge Medieval Studies 20*, 1-20

For traditions of Caswallawn, Maxen Wledic, and Arthur, see Bromwich, 274-7, 300-1, 451-4.

For traditions of Fionn mac Cumhaill, Cú Roi, and Cú Chulainn, see Ó hÓgáin (1990), 131-42, 203-8, 213-23.

BIBLIOGRAPHY

Most of the Classical Greek and Latin texts are edited with translation in the Loeb Classical Library series. Many of the texts are also published in translation in the Penguin Classics series. The following is a list of analytical works referred to in the notes.

Arbois de Jubainville, H d', *Sur l'Histoire des Celtes* (Paris, 1902)

Binchy, Daniel A, *Celtic and Anglo-Saxon Kingship* (Oxford, 1970)

Bromwich, Rachel, *Trioedd Ynys Prydein* (Cardiff, 1961)

Byrne, Francis John, *Irish Kings and High-Kings* (New York, 1973)

Cambridge Medieval Celtic Studies (Cambridge, 1981-)

Collingwood, R G / Myres, J N L, *Roman Britain and the English Settlements* (Oxford, 1937)

Cunliffe, Barry, *The Ancient Celts* (Oxford, 1997)

Dillon, Myles, *Celt and Hindu* (Dublin, 1973)

Dinan, W, *Monumenta Historica Celtica* (London, 1911)

Dottin, Georges, *Manuel de l'Antiquité Celtique* (Paris, 1915)

Eliade, Mircea, ed., *The Encyclopaedia of Religion 1-16* (New York, 1987)

Ellis, Peter Berresford, *The Celtic Empire* (London, 1990)

Ériu (Dublin, 1904-)

Falk Hjalmar/Torp, Alf, *Wortschatz der germanischen Spracheinheit* (Göttingen, 1979)

Filip, Jan, *Celtic Civilisation and its Heritage* (Prague, 1977)

Graves, Robert, *The Greek Myths 1-2* (Middlesex, 1960)

Holder, Alfred, *Alt-Celtischer Sprachschatz 1-3* (Leipzig, 1896)

Hubert, Henri, *The Greatness and Decline of the Celts* (London, 1987)

Irische Texte 1-4 (Leipzig, 1890-1909)

Jackson, Kenneth Hurlstone, *The Oldest Irish Tradition* (Cambridge, 1964); *Cath Maighe Léna* (Dublin, 1938)

Journal of Indo-European Studies (Hattiesburg, 1973-)

Jullian, Camille, *Histoire de la Gaule 1-8* (Paris, 1920-1926)

Kendrick, T D, *The Druids* (London, 1927)

King, Anthony, *Roman Gaul and Germany* (London, 1990)

Knott, Eleanor, *Togail Bruidne Da Derga* (Dublin, 1936)

Lambert, Pierre-Yves, *La Langue Gauloise* (Paris, 1994)

le Roux, Francoise/Guyonvarc'h, Christian-J, *Les Druides* (Ouest-France, 1986)

Lemprière, J, *Classical Dictionary* (London, 1984 ed)

Mac an Bhaird, Alan, 'Ptolemy Revisited' in *Ainm - Bulletin of the Ulster Place-Name Society*, 5 (1991-1993), 1-20

Ni Chatháin, Próinséas/Richter, Michael, eds., *Ireland and Europe in the early Middle Ages* (Stuttgart, 1996)

Ó hÓgáin, Dáithí, *Myth, Legend and Romance* (London, 1990)

Ogam (Rennes, 1948-)

O'Rahilly, Thomas F, *Early Irish History and Mythology* (Dublin, 1946)

Otia Merseiana 1-4 (Liverpool, 1899-1904)

Piggott, Stuart, *The Druids* (London, 1968)

Powell, T G E, *The Celts* (London, 1958)

Rankin, David, *Celts and the Classical World* (London, 1987)

Revue Celtique 1-55 (Paris, 1870-1934)

Rivet, A L F/Smith, Colin, *The Place-Names of Roman Britain* (London, 1979).

Ross, Anne, *Pagan Celtic Britain* (London, 1967)

Tierney, J J, 'The Celtic Ethnography of Posidonius' in *Proceedings of the Royal Irish Academy* 60 C5 (1960), 189-275.

Todd, Malcolm, *Roman Britain* (London, 1981)

Ua Riain, Eoin, *Féil-sgribhinn Eoin Mhic Néill* (Dublin, 1940)

Vries, Jan de, *Keltische Religion* (Stuttgart, 1961)

Wainwright, F T, ed., *The Problem of the Picts* (Edinburgh, 1955)

Walde, Alois/Pokorny, Julius, *Vergleichendes Wörterbuch der Indogermanischen Sprachen 1-2* (Berlin, 1927-1930)

Whatmough, Joshua, *The Dialects of Ancient Gaul* (Harvard, 1970)

Wikander, Stig, *Der arische Männerbund* (Lund, 1938)

Winbolt, S E, *Britain under the Romans* (Middlesex, 1945)

INDEX